gather

gather

MEMORABLE MENUS FOR ENTERTAINING THROUGHOUT THE SEASONS

Georgeanne Brennan
photography by Lara Hata *styling by* Ethel Brennan

SASQUATCH BOOKS
SEATTLE

Printed in China
Published by Sasquatch Books
Distributed by PGW/Perseus
15 14 13 12 11 10 09   9 8 7 6 5 4 3 2 1

Cover photograph (front left): Jim Henkens/www.jimhenkens.com
Cover photographs (front right & back): Lara Hata
Cover and interior design: Kate Basart/Union Pageworks
Interior photographs: Lara Hata
Photograph styling: Ethel Brennan

Library of Congress Cataloging-in-Publication Data

Brennan, Georgeanne
  Gather : memorable menus for entertaining throughout the seasons / Georgeanne
Brennan ; photography by Lara Hata ; styling by Ethel Brennan.
     p. cm.
  Includes index.
  ISBN-13: 978-1-57061-578-8
  ISBN-10: 1-57061-578-0
  1. Entertaining. 2. Cookery. I. Title.
  TX731.B6685 2009
  642—dc22
                              2009009216

SASQUATCH BOOKS
119 South Main Street, Suite 400 | Seattle, WA 98104 | 206-467-4300
www.sasquatchbooks.com | custserv@sasquatchbooks.com

To Oona, Oscar, and Raphael, the latest generation to come to our table, and to their parents, Oliver Brennan and Liz Valentine, Ethel Brennan and Laurent Rigobert—may we and all the rest of our extended family and friends gather together to share many, many more meals.

contents

acknowledgments

First, foremost, and always, to my husband, Jim Schrupp, my biggest fan, who reads everything I write, and without whom there would be only a small garden. Thanks to Tom and Katie Schrupp and Dan Schrupp for cheerfully sampling so much food in my kitchen and from our garden over the years, and for becoming such good cooks and gardeners themselves. Ethel, a special thanks to you for your inspired food and prop styling, and for the good advice you gave me about this book when I would go astray. And thanks for the fun we had working on this project together. Thank you, Lara, for the gorgeous photos and the way you captured the special light of every season. Thank you to Elise Revert for her calm, French demeanor while food styling. A very special thanks to my friend Melanie Bajakian who, when called on short notice to help with the wedding shoot, produced a carload of still-wrapped presents, party favors, platters, and trays from her daughter's wedding the week before, and for producing a three-tiered chocolate wedding cake from her restaurant, the Putah Creek Cafe. And to Yvonne, who made the cake.

Thanks to my agent, Danielle Svetcov, who pushed me to write several versions of the proposal, and to Gary Luke, publisher at Sasquatch Books, who patiently waited until I produced a proposal for the book he had in mind.

—GB

Thank you to Maison d'Etre (www.maisondetre.com) for letting us use so many of their beautiful props. Thank you to Elise Ravet for her help, use of her home, and for her beautiful food styling. Thank you to Heidi Hildenbrand-Goodman for joining in the styling fun; a very special thank you to Melanie Bajakian for her very generous contributions to our wedding-menu shoot. We would also like to thank Yvonne Galloway at the Putah Creek Cafe in Winters, California, for the delicious chocolate wedding cake! Thank you to Berryessa Gap Winery in Winters, California, for the use of their vineyards—one of our favorite locations.

—*LH & EB*

introduction

If I close my eyes I can see it. We're all in the kitchen, everyone helping. Mary Ann, a longtime friend and cooking co-conspirator, is filling *gougères* with the lobster salad she has made that morning. My daughter, Ethel, and two of her girlfriends from San Francisco are cracking open the roasted chestnuts for the soup. My son, Oliver, is grinding peppercorns with a pestle in the wooden mortar I brought from France many years ago, and my stepsons, Tom and Dan, are filling Belgian endive leaves with dabs of goat cheese, finishing them off with bits of smoked salmon and green peppercorns, and arranging them on a tray. My husband is adding another oak log to the kitchen fireplace, and a waft of wood smoke mingles with the rich aroma of the cassoulet in the oven. Katie, our friend from England, opens the Champagne and starts pouring it into flutes, just as the last *gougère* is filled. We raise our glasses in a toast. The occasion? An opportunity to be together.

Ten years later, my kitchen ranks have swollen to include two daughters-in-law, a son-in-law, and three grandchildren. The girlfriends are back, this time with husbands and children. Mary Ann, alas, is in Australia, but I think of her once again, as family and friends gather together in my kitchen, spilling out into the dining room, sipping Champagne as we put the finishing touches on a special meal. The occasion this time? Katie is back in town.

Life is full of occasions for celebrating, but too often we postpone them, thinking we're so busy that we don't have enough time or energy to plan and execute the party in our mind's eye. Sometimes this is true, such as the time I gave a pre–wedding dinner party for my stepson and his bride-to-be. More than fifty people were invited. I'd had my menu planned for weeks—gazpacho, paellas, green salad, and oven-roasted peaches with ice cream— and I had even hired someone to help me in the kitchen that evening. On the day of the party, the peaches I had ordered arrived hard as rocks, and while most of the food was ready, some of the details were missing. A friend helped me shop for the salad greens, picked up my seafood, adjusted the seasoning on the gazpacho for me, organized some helpers to peel and poach the peaches, finished the bouquets for the tables, and sent me to dress and have a glass of wine before the guests arrived. After a slightly stiff beginning, the two extended families and their friends cooked the paellas over the three grills I had lined up against the grape arbor, the wine and conversation flowed freely, and it turned out to be a memorable evening for all of us. In the end, it didn't matter that I hadn't rubbed every single toast with garlic, that I had forgotten to serve the olives, or that the party began with the wrong wine being poured.

A celebration doesn't need to be grand or large. It can be as simple as a housewarming for a friend or a new neighbor, a special meal for a book club or a movie night with friends. Celebrations are occasions to bring people together over good food, where the shared memories that are the basis of family, friendship, and community are created. Sometimes the occasion is a culturally acknowledged one, such as Thanksgiving or Christmas, a wedding or a birthday, but it can also be personal or quirky, like a summer solstice party, a dinner for the Day of the Dead, or an Easter egg–decorating party. For thousands of years people have celebrated the harvest, welcoming the new crops that will ensure that year's sustenance, so why not a Vintner's Feast, celebrating the grape harvest? Personally, I think a cozy Sunday supper, even for only four or five people, is one of the most enjoyable of occasions; and best of all, there are fifty-two Sundays in a year.

There are ways to make entertaining fun instead of stressful or time-consuming. I have learned a lot from my friends and neighbors in the south of France, where I have had a house for many years. They don't prepare every single dish for an entire meal. They focus on one or two items and purchase the rest. For example, appetizers are often simple: olives, nuts, toasts with a spread or a topping. The first course might be a composed salad, easy to prepare, followed by the main course and a beautiful dessert from the local patisserie. The host or hostess is free to focus his or her creative energy on cooking the main course.

Part of the fun of entertaining for me is choosing the table linens, flatware, and glassware; deciding on the decorations; and then assembling them all a day or two before the party. This takes a bit of doing to pull everything together, so I try to prepare well in advance. I usually set the table the morning of the party, or even the evening before. I prefer to keep the decorations simple and casual, focusing on the foliage, flowers, fruits, and nuts that are seasonally available, much of them harvested from my landscape and garden. Doing the table planning and executing it well ahead leaves me plenty of time to devote to cooking. And of course, whenever possible, and especially for larger gatherings, choosing dishes that can be prepared ahead, even frozen, is very helpful and eases the flow of the event.

This book reflects my personal style of entertaining—essentially simple, in season, and reflective of the natural world around me. I revel in the pleasure of acquiring quality ingredients, whether from my garden, farmers markets, friends who hunt or fish, or good purveyors. Fresh, seasonal fruits, vegetables, herbs, fish, and meats excite and inspire me with their promise. It's my job to celebrate the ingredients, not overwhelm them. That's both the challenge and the satisfaction.

For each menu in this book, I suggest ways to simplify the cooking and, in some instances, how to make a simple meal more grand. I also suggest, where appropriate, which dishes can be made ahead of time and how far ahead. The menus are grouped seasonally, beginning with spring, but you can adapt them to different seasons by substituting ingredients.

Decorating is highly personal, reflecting our individual sense of what is pleasing and what is beautiful. My daughter, Ethel, who is a prop and food stylist, favors clean, simple, contemporary looks. Her autumn table might have a single orchid in a clear glass vase and a natural linen table runner on a bare walnut table set with pale apple green–plates and sleek stainless steel. My table would likely be covered with heavy antique white French linen; overlaid with a square tablecloth of woven magenta, burnt orange, and deep gold; set with my mother's silver and an eclectic collection of dishes my husband has brought home to me over the years; and, in a low, glass bowl, graced with the last of my garden's dark-red roses. So while I do make some decorating suggestions throughout the book, they are meant to inspire rather than dictate.

I hope this book will help you discover and guide your own sensibilities, based on where you live and what grows around you; and above all, that it will encourage you to share your love of good food, family, and friends on every possible occasion, large or small.

spring

a sunday lunch in honor of parents

FRESH RICOTTA AND GREEN-GARLIC SPREAD

YOUNG RADISHES WITH BUTTER AND SEA SALT

CIDER-GLAZED CORNISH GAME HENS

CREAMY POLENTA WITH WHITE CHEDDAR AND GREEN ONIONS

SPRING CARROTS AND SUGAR SNAP PEAS BRAISED IN BUTTER

FRESH CHERRY COBBLER

*table setting for a sunday
lunch in honor of parents*

the party

Honoring parents with a special Sunday lunch, whether it's for Mother's Day, Father's Day, or just any Sunday, is a simple way to bring family and friends together. In Provence, Sunday lunch is the most important time of the week, an occasion to gather friends and family around the table for a long, leisurely meal brimming with conviviality and conversation. The food is carefully prepared but not elaborate, featuring whatever is in season. In spring, asparagus, artichokes, and strawberries are on the table, but in summer you'll find tomatoes and eggplant, in fall wild mushrooms, and, if you're lucky, truffles in winter.

At home in California, I give Sunday lunches for special occasions, and when that includes my husband Jim's family—seven siblings, all with spouses and children—it means lunch for thirty-five people. But whether Sunday lunch includes the whole extended family or just a handful, everyone lingers under our big black walnut tree, sipping wine and talking.

Decorating tips: Search for unusual, decorative picture frames and make a display of favorite family photos. Set them on a table for everyone to enjoy. Scan a photo of each family member as a child, and glue or tape it to that person's place card. If you have a garden with roses, ask a florist to make wristlets for the girls and women using your roses and rosebuds.

Cooking tips: If there's someone in the family who is a great pie-maker, assign that person the dessert. You could also purchase a spiral-cut ham instead of roasting the game hens. For a more elaborate lunch, you could add extra appetizers and serve ice cream with the cobbler.

fresh ricotta and green-garlic spread

This is a springtime version of a spread I make with shallots at other times of the year. The mild green garlic gives the spread a garlicky flavor that is fresh and not overpowering. Use soft, fluffy fresh ricotta, and if you can't find green garlic, substitute green onions.

Cut off the dark green leaves of the garlic and discard. Peel back and discard the tough outer leaves surrounding the garlic bulbs. Mince the tender bulbs and put the garlic into a small bowl. Add the cheese and salt and mix well with a fork. If the mixture seems too thick to spread, add a little cream. Cover and refrigerate for up to 6 hours.

To serve, put the spread on the toasts and sprinkle each with some of the garlic chives.

MAKES 16 APPETIZERS, ENOUGH FOR 8 SERVINGS

6 to 8 stalks green garlic

6 ounces fresh ricotta cheese, or 4 ounces fresh, soft goat cheese mixed with 4 tablespoons heavy cream

Pinch of sea salt

1 baguette, cut into 16 slices and toasted

2 tablespoons snipped fresh garlic chives (optional)

young radishes with butter and sea salt

young radishes with butter and sea salt

Often after I serve this dish—and I serve it only when the radishes are young and tender—people will remember it years later. It is the essence of springtime eating in Provence, where white-tablecloth restaurants and country homes alike honor these early, perfect vegetables. I grow successive plantings of radishes in my garden, and I use them throughout the spring. Choose small, crisp radishes, preferably of the French Breakfast variety, which are oblong with white tips. Serve this with coarse sea salt (gray is my personal favorite), sweet butter, and slices of baguette.

Clean the radishes, leaving intact the small roots and several of the green leaves. Put the radishes in a bowl of ice water and refrigerate for several hours. This will make them nice and crisp. When ready to serve, pat them dry, arrange them on a platter, and bring them to the table with the butter, salt, and bread, and a bowl for the discarded leaves.

Diners help themselves to butter and salt, spreading some butter on the radish and dipping it in the salt. The butter helps the salt adhere to the radish, and the combination, along with the baguette, is delectable.

MAKES 8 SERVINGS

1 or 2 bunches small radishes, preferably the white-tipped French Breakfast variety
½ cup (1 stick) unsalted butter, at room temperature
¼ cup coarse sea salt
1 baguette, cut into thin slices

cider-glazed cornish game hens

I have always been a fan of these small birds. Glazing them makes their delicate skin gleam and infuses them with flavor. Cut into halves or even quarters, Cornish game hens are just right for a spring lunch. Apple juice is too sweet for the glaze, so do choose fresh apple cider.

In a small bowl, combine the apple cider, brown sugar, soy sauce, ginger, mustard, and vinegar and mix well. Put the birds in a large zip-top bag and pour in the apple cider mixture. Close the bag and refrigerate for 2 hours.

Preheat the oven to 350°F.

Remove the birds from the bag, reserving the juices, and place them cut side down on a rack in a shallow roasting pan. Sprinkle the birds with the salt and pepper, and put 2 sprigs of thyme under each one. Roast for 30 to 40 minutes, until golden, then baste several times with the reserved juices. Continue to cook until the inner thigh can be easily pierced with the tip of a knife and the juices run clear, about another 10 minutes. Discard any remaining marinade.

Remove the birds from the oven and let them stand, loosely covered with foil, for 10 to 15 minutes. Arrange them on a platter garnished with the remaining thyme sprigs. Serve hot.

MAKES 8 SERVINGS

¼ cup apple cider

½ cup firmly packed brown sugar

1 teaspoon soy sauce

1 teaspoon peeled, minced fresh gingerroot

1 teaspoon Dijon mustard

1 tablespoon cider vinegar

4 Cornish game hens, halved lengthwise

½ teaspoon coarse sea salt or kosher salt

½ teaspoon freshly ground black pepper

16 to 20 sprigs fresh thyme

cider-glazed cornish game hens, spring carrots and sugar snap peas braised in butter, and creamy polenta with white cheddar and green onions

creamy polenta with white cheddar and green onions

I serve creamy polenta often throughout the year, sometimes adding a taste of whatever is in season, such as green onions in spring, bell peppers in summer, and wild mushrooms in fall.

Finely chop the green onions, using all but the upper third of the green stalk. Melt 1 tablespoon of the butter in a frying pan over medium heat. Add the green onions and let them "sweat," cooking them through but not letting them brown, about 5 minutes. Remove them from the heat and set aside.

In a large saucepan over medium-high heat, bring 4 cups of the water to a boil. Add the polenta in a steady stream, whisking as you pour it into the pot. Whisk in the salt.

Reduce the heat to low and continue whisking until there are no lumps, about 5 minutes. Continue to cook until the polenta is soft, has thickened, and begins to pull away from the sides of the pan, about 20 minutes. (Add more water if the polenta gets thick before it is soft enough.) Stir in the remaining butter, the cheese, pepper, and green onions. Serve immediately.

MAKES 8 SERVINGS

1 bunch green onions
4 tablespoons (½ stick) unsalted butter, divided
6 to 7 cups water
1½ cups polenta
1 teaspoon coarse sea salt or kosher salt
⅓ cup shredded white cheddar cheese or soft, fresh goat cheese
½ teaspoon freshly ground white pepper

spring carrots and sugar snap peas braised in butter

Young carrots and peas, along with fava beans, symbolize spring for me, and I consider them to be very special. I usually grow carrots in my spring garden, but I tend to buy peas because of the garden space they require. Whenever they are available, I buy English shelling peas and use them along with or instead of the sugar snaps, adding them to the pan at the same time. This dish, like the polenta, needs to be cooked just before serving.

Trim and peel the carrots, leaving about ½ inch of the greens intact. Cut the carrots in half lengthwise, then in half again crosswise, on an angle.

Melt 1 tablespoon of the butter in a sauté pan or frying pan over medium heat. When it foams, add the carrots and sprinkle them with the salt. Turn them several times, then cover the pan tightly and reduce the heat to low.

Braise for 5 minutes, then add the remaining butter and 2 teaspoons of the broth. Cover and cook until the carrots are nearly tender, for about 5 more minutes. Add the sugar snap peas and a little more broth if needed, and cook for 3 to 4 minutes. Serve immediately.

MAKES 8 SERVINGS

1 or 2 bunches (about 16 to 20) slender young carrots with their green tops attached

1½ tablespoons unsalted butter, divided

¼ teaspoon coarse sea salt or kosher salt

2 to 4 teaspoons chicken or vegetable broth

1½ pounds sugar snap peas, trimmed and cut in half crosswise

peonies for a sunday lunch in honor
of parents table decoration

fresh cherry cobbler

I have a Montmorency sour cherry tree in my front yard. These cherries make the best pies and cobblers imaginable, with just the right amount of tartness to make you want more and more. However, the window of harvest time is short, so during the rest of the cherry season, I use purchased bing, Royal Ann, or other cherry varieties. Fresh cherry cobbler is worth the pitting, which can be done the day before.

Preheat the oven to 425°F.

Put the sugar, the 5 tablespoons of flour, and the cherries in a bowl. Turn several times, mixing well. Let stand for 15 to 20 minutes.

Sift together the remaining flour, salt, and baking powder. With a pastry cutter or 2 knives, cut 2 tablespoons of the butter into the flour mixture until pea-size grains form. Pour in ⅓ cup of the milk and mix with a fork to make a slightly stiff dough. If it is too stiff, add a little more milk, but do not overmix the dough.

Turn the dough out onto a well-floured work surface and pat or roll it out into a square about ½ inch thick.

Lightly grease a 9-inch square baking dish with ½ teaspoon of butter and pour the cherry mixture into it. Cut the remaining butter in small pieces and dot the cherries with the bits. Lay the pastry dough on top. Don't worry if there are rough edges or if a little of the filling shows through.

Bake until the filling is bubbling and the crust is puffed and golden brown, about 30 minutes.

Remove the cobbler from the oven and let it stand for at least 20 minutes or up to 2 hours before serving. Serve the cobbler hot, warm, or at room temperature.

MAKES 8 SERVINGS

1¼ cups sugar (¾ cup if using sweet cherries)
¾ cup plus 5 tablespoons all-purpose flour
6 cups fresh sour or sweet cherries, pitted
½ teaspoon fine sea salt or kosher salt
1½ teaspoons baking powder
3 tablespoons unsalted butter, chilled, divided
⅓ to ½ cup milk

a neighborhood brunch

HOT POPOVERS WITH ORANGE-SCENTED CREAM CHEESE

HOMEMADE PORK SAUSAGE PATTIES WITH SAGE

BAKED EGG SCRAMBLE WITH WHITE CHEDDAR AND AVOCADO

BABY SPINACH SALAD WITH RED ONION, FETA, AND STRAWBERRIES

the party

Aweekend brunch is a good time to get the neighbors together, leaving everyone time for the rest of their busy weekend. I usually invite people for brunch around 10:30 a.m., so this menu leans more toward breakfast than lunch, but I like to give a nod to lunch with a seasonal salad. I prepare some dishes, such as the homemade sausage and the orange-scented cream cheese, the day before. The popovers go in the oven at 10 a.m. When guests arrive, I offer them coffee, juice, or a mimosa. While they enjoy their drinks, I cook the sausage and the egg dish, and then brunch is ready to serve, with the popovers hot from the oven.

Decorating tips: Because some of the guests might not yet be acquainted, set the table with place cards decorated with a sprig of rosemary or other fresh herb, and be sure to include a bouquet of spring flowers, such as tulips, daffodils, or freesias.

Cooking tips: If time is running short, buy the sausage and sprinkle it with a little minced fresh sage. If you're feeling especially festive, throw together a pitcher of mimosas at the last minute.

hot popovers with
orange-scented cream cheese

Popovers are so versatile and easy, they deserve to make a comeback in our kitchens. They are light and airy, a perfect foil for sweet jams and cheeses, but they are equally receptive to savory toppings, such as braised beef and leeks. The batter is the same as the batter for Yorkshire pudding. For this menu, I serve them with a citrusy cream cheese spread. Blackberry jam makes a great addition.

Preheat the oven to 475°F.

Combine the flour, salt, sugar, milk, melted butter, and eggs and beat with a whisk or an electric mixer until thoroughly blended, 2 to 3 minutes. Grease a 12-cup muffin tin with the butter. Place the tin in the oven for 5 minutes to heat, then remove it and fill each cup ½ to ¾ full with the batter.

Bake the popovers for 15 minutes, then reduce the heat to 350°F and bake until the popovers are deeply browned and puffed, about 20 minutes. Remove them from the oven and serve immediately with the Orange-Scented Cream Cheese and the blackberry jam, if desired.

MAKES 12 POPOVERS, ENOUGH FOR 6 TO 8 SERVINGS

1¼ cups all-purpose flour
½ teaspoon coarse sea salt or
   kosher salt
½ teaspoon sugar
1 cup whole milk
1 tablespoon unsalted butter,
   melted
2 eggs
1 tablespoon unsalted butter for
   greasing pan
Orange-Scented Cream Cheese
   (recipe follows)
Blackberry jam (optional)

hot popovers with
orange-scented cream cheese

orange-scented cream cheese

Mash the cream cheese with the back of a fork in a bowl. Add the orange zest, orange juice, and sugar and continue to mash and mix until well blended. Transfer the cream cheese to a serving bowl and cover tightly. The spread can be made up to 24 hours ahead of time and refrigerated. To serve, bring the spread to room temperature.

MAKES 1 CUP, ENOUGH FOR 6 TO 8 SERVINGS

8 ounces cream cheese, at room temperature
Zest of 1 medium-size orange (2 to 3 tablespoons)
2 tablespoons freshly squeezed orange juice
1 teaspoon sugar

homemade pork sausage patties with sage

Making homemade sausage patties is easy if you use a food processor. Pulsing the cubed meat in the processor produces much the same result as grinding it. Pork butt is a good choice for sausages because it has a good ratio of fat to meat. Too little fat means the sausages will be dry. You can season the meat with salt, pepper, and other spices, and use herbs of your choice. The patties can be made ahead and frozen, then used at your convenience, or you can cook them fresh. They will keep in the refrigerator, well-wrapped, for up to five days.

Working in batches, put the pork in the bowl of a food processor fitted with the steel blade and pulse a few times until coarsely ground. Transfer the pork to a large bowl.

In a small spice grinder or clean coffee grinder, or using a mortar and pestle, grind the coriander, fennel, and peppercorns together until finely ground. Add them to the pork, along with the salt, cayenne, and sage, and mix well, using your hands or a wooden spoon, to evenly distribute the ingredients. Shape the mixture into patties about 4 inches in diameter and ½ inch thick.

Heat the olive oil in a large skillet over medium-high heat. Add the sausage patties, in batches if necessary, and cook them until the bottoms have browned, 3 to 4 minutes. Turn them and cook the other side until browned, another 3 to 4 minutes. Remove the patties to a paper towel to drain. Serve hot.

MAKES 6 TO 8 SERVINGS

1¾ to 2 pounds boneless pork butt, cut into 2-inch pieces
2 teaspoons whole coriander seed
1 teaspoon whole fennel seed
2 teaspoons whole black peppercorns
1½ teaspoons sea salt or kosher salt
¼ teaspoon cayenne
3 tablespoons finely chopped fresh sage
3 tablespoons extra-virgin olive oil

baked egg scramble with white cheddar and avocado

Finishing the eggs in the oven gives a few minutes of breathing space to the cook, which I always appreciate. You can substitute other cheeses here, such as fontina, other cheddars, or Gouda, and you can vary the fresh herbs according to your taste and what is available. The avocados make a pretty as well as flavorful garnish.

Preheat the oven to 400°F.

Crack the eggs into a bowl and beat them with a fork or whisk. Add the salt, pepper, and cream and beat again to blend. In a large ovenproof frying pan, melt the butter over medium-high heat. When it foams, add the eggs, scrambling them with a fork. As soon as they begin to form curds, after about 1 minute, stir in the cheese and put the pan in the oven until the curds are set, another 3 to 5 minutes, depending upon whether you like your eggs soft or firm.

Remove the eggs to a warm platter or individual plates and garnish with the avocado slices.

MAKES 8 SERVINGS

12 eggs
½ teaspoon coarse sea salt or kosher salt
½ teaspoon cracked pink peppercorns or freshly ground black pepper
2 tablespoons heavy cream
2 tablespoons unsalted butter
4 ounces (1 cup) white cheddar cheese, shredded
2 avocados, peeled, pitted, and cut into ¼-inch-thick slices

baby spinach salad with red onion, feta, and strawberries

The first time I made this, I had a lot of extra strawberries on hand, and I wanted to make something savory rather than sweet. I thought, why not add the strawberries to a spinach salad? The white balsamic softens the vinegar just a bit and takes the edge off the spinach. Regular balsamic could be used as well, but it will darken the spinach and feta.

Cut the onion into thin slices, then cut the slices crosswise to make quarter-moons. In a salad bowl, mix together the olive oil, red wine vinegar, balsamic vinegar, salt, and pepper. Add the onions and the strawberries and mix gently several times. Add the baby spinach and the feta cheese. The salad can sit as is, without tossing, for up to 30 minutes. When ready to serve, toss well.

MAKES 8 SERVINGS

¼ medium-size red onion

3 tablespoons extra-virgin olive oil

2 tablespoons red wine vinegar

1 teaspoon white balsamic vinegar

¼ teaspoon coarse sea salt or kosher salt

¼ teaspoon freshly ground black pepper

1 pint strawberries, hulled and quartered

5 cups baby spinach leaves

6 ounces feta cheese, crumbled

easter egg–decorating party

DEVILED EGGS

OVEN-ROASTED ASPARAGUS WITH TANGERINE AÏOLI

DUNGENESS CRAB CAKE GRATIN

WATERCRESS AND BUTTERHEAD LETTUCE SALAD

STRAWBERRIES WITH POUND CAKE AND WHIPPED CREAM

*table decorations for an
easter egg–decorating party*

the party

When I discovered that Santa Claus, the tooth fairy, and the Easter Bunny weren't real, I asked my mother to promise us that the Easter Bunny would always come, no matter what. So, well into our teens, my brother and I hunted for Easter eggs, even after we had begun dyeing them ourselves. I continued this ritual with my own children, rewarding them after for their hard work with a party. With this menu I like to pour Prosecco for the adults to sip as they nibble their deviled eggs, then serve the asparagus, gratin, and salad together, followed by the strawberries and pound cake.

Decorating tips: On a side table I put a collection of Easter baskets filled with fresh grass or straw, plus a chocolate rabbit or two, along with my antique chocolate rabbit mold and a bouquet of flowering spring bulbs, perhaps freesias or ranunculus in a riot of Easter egg pastels. The dining table centerpiece might be a grass-filled basket that shows off the newly decorated eggs, and some short candles, interwoven with ivy.

Cooking tips: To simplify this menu, you could skip the salad. For a more elaborate dinner party, serve the asparagus as a separate course, add a cheese course before the dessert, and make some homemade meringues for the strawberries instead of buying the pound cake.

deviled eggs

deviled eggs

This is a purist's version of deviled eggs, the way I learned to make them from my neighbors in Provence, with no additions to the mashed egg yolk other than salt, pepper, Dijon mustard, and a little bit of mayonnaise—just enough to fluff up the yolks. If you'd like a little extra color, sprinkle the eggs with snipped chives, parsley, or paprika. When I serve these, I bring out the glass deviled-egg serving dish that was my mother's.

Put the eggs in a saucepan, cover them with cold water, and bring the water to a boil over high heat. As soon as the water boils, remove the pan from the heat and cover it. Let the eggs stand for 20 minutes, then remove them from the pan and rinse under cold water. Peel the eggs, then cut them in half lengthwise. Gently remove the yolks and transfer them to a bowl. Using a fork, mash the yolks with the mustard, salt, and pepper, then add the mayonnaise and blend well. With a teaspoon, fill each half-egg cavity with some of the yolk mixture.

Arrange the romaine leaves on a platter, and place the deviled eggs on top.

MAKES 12 APPETIZERS, ENOUGH FOR 4 TO 6 SERVINGS

6 eggs
1 tablespoon Dijon mustard
½ teaspoon coarse sea salt or kosher salt
½ teaspoon freshly ground white pepper
2 tablespoons mayonnaise
Romaine lettuce leaves for garnish

oven-roasted asparagus with tangerine aïoli

The asparagus in our kitchen garden is in full production in March and April—perfect timing for Easter. Although we eat it almost every day throughout its season, it is so sweet and tender that I never get tired of it. I can harvest the asparagus just before I cook it, which is really a luxury. Usually, I simply steam or sauté it, but roasting the asparagus adds to the flavor, and the faint smokiness is a good match with the citrusy sweetness of the aïoli. If you can't find tangerine-infused olive oil, substitute orange or lemon. The aïoli can be made in the morning and kept refrigerated for several days, but remember, it becomes stronger with each passing day.

2 pounds asparagus, trimmed

2½ tablespoons extra-virgin olive oil

1½ teaspoons coarse sea salt or kosher salt, divided

5 cloves garlic

3 egg yolks

1½ cups tangerine-infused extra-virgin olive oil

Preheat the oven to 450°F.

Place the asparagus spears in a single, snug layer in a shallow baking dish; use two dishes if necessary. Sprinkle the asparagus with the olive oil and about half (¾ teaspoon) of the salt. Turn the spears several times to coat them, then roast them, uncovered, until the tips become tinged with gold, about 15 to 20 minutes. Remove the pan from the oven and arrange the spears on a platter.

To prepare the aïoli, put the remaining salt into a mortar or other small bowl, along with the garlic. Using a pestle or the back of a wooden spoon, grind and pound the salt and garlic together to make a paste.

Transfer the paste to a mixing bowl and add the egg yolks, whisking to incorporate them. Slowly drizzle in the infused olive oil, literally drop by drop, whisking constantly, or use an electric mixer. Gradually the paste will thicken; at this point you can add the remaining oil in a steady but very thin stream. Continue whisking or beating until all the oil has been incorporated and you have achieved a loose mayonnaise-like consistency.

Serve the asparagus warm or at room temperature, accompanied by the aïoli.

MAKES 6 SERVINGS

dungeness crab cake gratin

I love Dungeness crab, and we eat it as often as possible when it is in season, which is winter through spring here in Northern California. Rather than making individual crab cakes for a group of people, I like to make a gratin. Adding grated cucumber and apple makes for a fluffy dish and also stretches the crab. My mother used to make a similar dish with canned crab, a favorite childhood food memory. She would serve it in large clamshells she had collected. If you clean the crabs the night before and cook the meat, it's easy to assemble and cook the gratin just before serving it.

Preheat the oven to 450°F.

Grate the cucumber using the large holes of a box grater, then squeeze out the liquid with your hands and put the grated cucumber in a bowl. Grate the apple the same way, squeeze out the liquid, and put the grated apple in the bowl.

Using 2 forks, shred the crab into large flakes and add to the bowl. Add the the chives, tarragon, olive oil, 4 tablespoons of the mayonnaise, salt, pepper, lemon juice, and cayenne. Mix well. The mixture should just hold together. If it does not, add more mayonnaise and mix to combine.

Butter a 3-cup shallow gratin dish. Spread the crab mixture into it and smooth the top. Sprinkle the panko over the top and drizzle with the melted butter.

Bake the gratin for 10 minutes, until warmed through, then place it under the broiler to brown the top, about 4 minutes.

Remove the gratin from the oven and serve hot in the baking dish.

MAKES 6 SERVINGS

½ small cucumber, peeled and seeded (about ½ cup)

1 small green apple, peeled and cored (about ¾ cup)

Cooked crabmeat from 3 large Dungeness crabs (about 3½ to 4 cups)

1½ tablespoons snipped fresh chives

3 teaspoons minced fresh tarragon

½ teaspoon extra-virgin olive oil

4 to 5 tablespoons mayonnaise

½ to 1 teaspoon coarse sea salt or kosher salt

½ teaspoon freshly ground black pepper

2 teaspoons freshly squeezed lemon juice

¼ teaspoon cayenne

1 teaspoon unsalted butter

¾ cup panko (Japanese bread crumbs)

4 tablespoons (½ stick) unsalted butter, melted

watercress and butterhead lettuce salad

I like this simple, slightly bitter salad with the sweet crab gratin, but you could use another mixture of greens instead. When my garden is full of spring lettuces, I use those, but growing lettuce in spring is often a battle between me and the birds, who like the young lettuces as much as I do and make attempts to swoop them up.

In a salad bowl, combine the olive oil and vinegar, mixing well with a fork. Add the salt and pepper and mix again. Add the watercress. Choose about a dozen of the small pale yellow and green inner leaves from the lettuce, and tear them into bite-size pieces. You should have about 3 cups of lettuce leaves. If not, continue selecting and tearing leaves until you do. Add these to the watercress, then add the parsley. Just before serving, toss well.

MAKES 6 SERVINGS

3 tablespoons extra-virgin olive oil

2 tablespoons Champagne vinegar

½ teaspoon coarse sea salt or kosher salt

½ teaspoon freshly ground black pepper

2 bunches watercress, stems removed (about 3 cups)

1 head butterhead lettuce, separated into leaves

¼ cup minced flat-leaf parsley

strawberries with pound cake and whipped cream

Since I will have put most of my energy into making the aïoli and the crab gratin, I'm going to buy the pound cake to serve with the strawberries. If the strawberries are a little bland, as they sometimes are early in the season, I'll toss them with some red wine and sugar before serving them. The whipped cream can be made several hours in advance, then covered and refrigerated until ready to use.

Whip the cream with an electric mixer until soft peaks form, about 5 minutes. Add the sugar and beat again for about 1 minute more.

Arrange 1 or 2 slices of cake on each of 6 dessert plates. Spoon some of the strawberries over the cake slices and top with several spoonfuls of whipped cream. Serve immediately.

MAKES 6 SERVINGS

1 cup heavy cream
2 tablespoons sugar
1 medium pound cake, cut into ½-inch slices
2 pints fresh, ripe strawberries, hulled and sliced

cinco de mayo

PORK CARNITAS

AVOCADO, ANCHO, AND PINEAPPLE SALSAS

SAVORY BLACK BEANS WITH ANCHO CHILES

CORN ON THE COB WITH QUESO FRESCO, CHILI POWDER, AND LIME

MANGO AND PAPAYA PALETAS

mango and papaya paletas

the party

Cinco de Mayo (May 5) commemorates the initial defeat of the French in their attempt to occupy Mexico in 1862, and it is an occasion for fiestas, piñatas, music, and lots of good food. Almost half the population of my town is of Latin American ancestry, so there are many Cinco de Mayo celebrations each year, and the mariachi music from town wafts across the creek to my house, linking my party to others.

A Cinco de Mayo celebration is a casual, fun party, and it doesn't require extensive or elaborate cooking. Guests can assemble their own tacos, sample the salsas, and fill their plates with homemade beans and grilled corn on the cob—but remind them to save room for dessert. Have plenty of chilled Mexican beer on ice, along with some fresh limeade.

Decorating tips: Set the table with red, green, and white—the national colors of Mexico. Hang several piñatas, to be knocked down later by children (or adults), and purchase small terra-cotta pots of succulent plants for the table setting—and then send them home with your guests when they depart.

Cooking tips: To simplify, purchase the salsas and use canned beans, punching up their flavor with the garlic and dried chiles, although if you haven't tried cooking dried beans from scratch, you'll be amazed at how much more flavorful they will be. You could also substitute purchased fruit pops for the homemade *paletas*. To expand the menu, add rice cooked in broth with cilantro.

pork carnitas

Carnitas, *pork that is slow-cooked in broth, then crisped and shredded, is authentic Mexican food. Locally, we see* carnitas *being cooked in kettles over open fires for celebrations, especially at harvest end, but* carnitas *are easy to make more conventionally in the kitchen. Choose a good-quality, bone-in pork shoulder for the best results. The* carnitas *can easily be made a day or two ahead of the party and reheated. If you do this, reserve some of the juices for the reheating.*

For the best-quality tortillas, look for them in a local Latin American market. In communities with a significant Latino population, there are often tortilla factories that sell freshly made tortillas retail. If you find some, be sure to buy them the day of the party. They are meant to be eaten fresh, and they are delicious. Plan on at least three tortillas per person, more if you have hungry teenagers.

5- to 6-pound bone-in pork shoulder
1½ tablespoons dried oregano
1 teaspoon cumin seeds
1½ teaspoons coarse sea salt or kosher salt
2 whole dried ancho chile peppers, or California or *pasilla* dried chiles
1 medium-size yellow onion, cut into quarters
2 cloves garlic, crushed
3½ cups chicken broth, water, or half broth, half water
Corn or flour tortillas, warmed

Preheat the oven to 350°F.

Rub the pork all over with the oregano, cumin seeds, and salt. Place it in a large, heavy Dutch oven and add the chile peppers, onion, and garlic. Cover the pork with the broth and bring it to a boil, spooning the liquid over the meat. Cover the Dutch oven and put it in the oven. Cook until the meat is pulling away from the bone and tender enough to be cut with a spoon, about 4 hours.

Return the Dutch oven to the stove top, skim off as much fat as possible, and discard the onion and chile peppers. If you plan to reheat the *carnitas* the next day, reserve ¼ cup of the juices and refrigerate.

Over medium-high heat, cook the meat, shredding it as it cooks. Continue to cook until the pan juices are gone and the meat is crisped and browned, only about 3 or 4 minutes longer. Remove the meat to a serving platter, discarding the bone. Cover the meat with foil to keep it warm until ready to serve. If you are reheating the *carnitas*, put the reserved pan juices and ¼ cup of water in a pan along with the meat, cover, and heat in the oven at 350°F until warmed through, about 30 minutes.

Serve the *carnitas* hot or warm, with flour tortillas and Avocado, Ancho, and Pineapple salsas.

MAKES 6 TO 8 SERVINGS

avocado salsa

Salsas are the essential condiment for Mexican food of all kinds, and while there are many types you can purchase, I prefer to serve homemade salsas.

A friend from Guanajuato, Mexico, taught me how to make this salsa, which combines tomatillos with avocados and is typically served with rich meats. It is so well liked that I can never make quite enough of it.

Remove the papery husks from the tomatillos. Place them in a large saucepan and cover by 2 inches with water. Over high heat, bring the water to a boil. Reduce the heat and cook the tomatillos until their color lightens, about 5 minutes. Drain and rinse under cold water. When the tomatillos are cool enough to handle, dice them and set aside.

Cut the chile peppers lengthwise, remove the seeds and ribs, then mince them. Combine the tomatillos, chiles, onion, garlic, and cilantro in a bowl. Cut the avocados into several chunks, then add them to the bowl. Mash everything together with the back of a fork, but leave the salsa chunky. Stir in the lime juice and the salt. Taste, and add more salt if necessary.

MAKES 2 CUPS, ENOUGH FOR 6 TO 8 SERVINGS

10 tomatillos
6 Hungarian wax chile peppers
4 serrano chile peppers
½ medium-size yellow onion, minced
2 cloves garlic, minced
8 sprigs fresh cilantro, minced
2 ripe avocados, peeled and pitted
Juice of 1 lime (1½ to 2 tablespoons)
½ teaspoon coarse sea salt or kosher salt

ancho salsa

This rich, dark salsa provides a visual and flavor contrast with Pineapple Salsa and Avocado Salsa. Toasting the chiles, tomatoes, and tomatillos gives it a smoky taste. Pumpkin seeds not only add another flavor but also thicken the sauce, a popular technique in Mexican cooking.

3 whole dried ancho chile peppers
1 cup hot water
¼ cup chopped fresh cilantro leaves
3 tomatillos, husks removed, cut in half crosswise
2 whole canned or fresh tomatoes
1 tablespoon hulled pumpkin seeds
½ teaspoon coarse sea salt or kosher salt
1 teaspoon safflower oil

Put the chile peppers on a griddle or in a dry skillet over medium heat, and toast them just long enough to make them supple, about 1 minute per side, pressing down on them with the back of a wooden spoon. Put them in a bowl, add the hot water, and let them stand for 15 minutes. Drain, reserving the water. Remove the stems, seeds, and veins, and coarsely chop the chile peppers.

Put the chiles in a blender with the cilantro and 2 tablespoons of the reserved water, and process to form a paste.

With the same griddle or skillet you used to toast the chile peppers, sear the tomatillos, skin side down, and the tomatoes, if using fresh, over medium heat, for 1 to 2 minutes.

Add the seared tomatillos and the canned or seared fresh tomatoes to the blender, along with the pumpkin seeds, salt, and oil. Purée to create a smooth sauce. Add some of the reserved water, a little at a time, until the sauce has the consistency of heavy cream.

MAKES 1 CUP, ENOUGH FOR 4 TO 6 SERVINGS

pineapple salsa

With its sweet taste of pineapple balanced by chiles, onion, and cilantro, this salsa is almost like a side salad. Like other fresh salsas, it is best served the day it is made.

Cut the chile peppers lengthwise, remove the seeds and the ribs, and then mince them. Combine the chile peppers, pineapple, red onion, cilantro, and chili powder in a bowl and mix well. Cover the salsa and refrigerate until ready to serve.

MAKES 2 CUPS, ENOUGH FOR 6 TO 8 SERVINGS

2 serrano chile peppers
1½ cups diced fresh pineapple
½ cup minced red onion
½ cup chopped fresh cilantro
  leaves
½ teaspoon chili powder

savory black beans with ancho chiles

These beans are best made the day before to allow the flavors to develop; then they are covered and refrigerated overnight.

Wash the beans and discard any broken ones. In a large, heavy-bottomed saucepan over medium-high heat, combine the beans, 8 cups of the water, onion, bay leaves, oregano sprigs, chiles, garlic, and salt and bring them to a boil. Reduce the heat to low, partially cover, and simmer until the beans are tender, 1½ to 2 hours. If the liquid evaporates, add a little more water.

Remove the pot from the heat and stir in the cayenne. Let the beans cool to room temperature. For a milder version, remove the chiles from the beans before refrigerating. The next day, remove the bay leaves, oregano sprigs, and the chiles, if left in. Reheat the beans over a low flame and taste for seasoning, adding more salt or cayenne, if desired. Stir in the dried oregano. Serve hot or at room temperature.

MAKES 8 SERVINGS

1 pound black beans
8 to 10 cups water
1 medium-size yellow onion, cut into quarters
2 bay leaves
6 sprigs fresh oregano
4 whole dried red chile peppers, such as ancho, Colorado, or poblano
4 cloves garlic, crushed
2 teaspoons salt
¼ to ½ teaspoon cayenne
1 teaspoon dried oregano

corn on the cob with queso fresco,
chili powder, and lime

corn on the cob with queso fresco, chili powder, and lime

This is a popular Mexican street food. I love the way the different vibrant flavors complement each other.

Build a wood or charcoal fire in a grill, or preheat a gas grill. Rub the corn with the oil. When the coals are hot or the grill reaches 400°F, place the corn on it, and turn it as it cooks. When the corn is lightly golden, about 6 minutes total, transfer it to a platter.

Sprinkle the corn with the cheese, chili powder, and cilantro, and garnish with the lime wedges. Serve hot.

MAKES 12 SERVINGS

12 ears corn, shucked

2 tablespoons corn or safflower oil

8 ounces *queso fresco* or other fresh crumbly cheese, or substitute mild feta

2 teaspoons chili powder

½ cup chopped fresh cilantro leaves

8 limes, cut into wedges

mango and papaya paletas

I buy mango and papaya juice and freeze it to prepare these frosty treats. These are two of my favorite tropical fruits, but you could certainly use other juices as well. If you have Popsicle molds, use those. They can be purchased at kitchenware stores, craft stores, or from specialty sources online. Or use small paper cups and skewers, but cut off the sharp tips of the skewers first.

Pour the fruit nectar into the Popsicle molds, filling them approximately three quarters full. Insert the Popsicle sticks and freeze until solid, approximately 6 hours or overnight. To unmold the Popsicles, dip the bottom of the molds briefly in a dish of hot water. Serve immediately.

MAKES APPROXIMATELY 22 PALETAS

45 ounces tropical or other fruit nectar or juice
Popsicle molds or small paper cups and wooden or bamboo skewers, sharp tips cut off

summer

a wedding to remember

BELGIAN ENDIVE WITH CRÈME FRAÎCHE AND SMOKED SALMON

GOUGÈRES FILLED WITH HERBED GOAT CHEESE

GRILLED LAMB AND RED PEPPER SKEWERS—OR—GRILLED HALIBUT AND
    YELLOW PEPPER SKEWERS

MIXED GRILLED SUMMER VEGETABLES

HEIRLOOM TOMATO PLATTER WITH PURPLE BASIL

FRESH SHELLING AND GREEN BEAN SALAD WITH WINTER SAVORY

SALAD OF MIXED GREENS

FROSTED SUGAR COOKIES

table setting for a wedding to remember

the party

When my daughter, Ethel, announced that she was getting married and wanted to hold the wedding at our house, I was thrilled. She then asked me to do the food with her. We would create the menu and order all the ingredients from the local farmers we've known and worked with over the years, and our friends and family would handle the actual cooking. As the guest list quickly grew to 250, I realized we needed a different approach. I didn't want to attempt cooking for that large a crowd, but Ethel and I agreed that the food had to be both personal and local.

So we worked with the only caterer in our small town, providing them with all the recipes and raw ingredients, and arranged for them to take over from there. Farmer friends delivered boxes of salad greens from the coast and flats of heirloom tomatoes, peppers, eggplant, and summer squash from just down the road. I picked the basil and other herbs from my garden, and we ordered halibut from Berkeley's Monterey Fish Market and boned leg of lamb from a packinghouse in nearby Dixon.

We did, however, do some of the cooking. Two days before the wedding, Ethel and I, along with a half dozen of her friends and her mother-in-law-to-be, made French onion soup to serve at midnight. All six of my stove's burners held pots simmering with ten recipes' worth of Julia Child's classic recipe. We toasted, then rubbed with garlic about a hundred slices of *pain au levain*, and we grated bowls and bowls of Parmesan and Emmentaler cheese.

Long after the caterers had driven away with their grills and the band had finally stopped playing, thirty or so remaining guests, including the musicians, gathered in the kitchen, while Ethel, barefoot in her white silk-satin wedding gown, ladled the soup into bowls.

Decorating tips: Weddings are inherently decorative, with their festive tables of Champagne glasses, flowers, place cards, crisp linens, and beribboned packages stacked high. For Ethel's wedding, she and her friends constructed rounds of flowing pink and gold streamers that were mounted on tall poles, where they fluttered in the evening breeze. We used flowers mostly from our garden, including sunflowers, roses, zinnias, and dahlias. Bouquets for the tables were made up the day before. For a personal touch, we asked the caterer to use our own collection of serving platters.

Although these are the menu and recipes we used, I've given quantities for ten servings, not 250. All the recipes can be easily scaled up four or five times. Beyond fifty guests, I call in a caterer, as that is my personal limit for entertaining on my own, even with help from family members and friends.

Cooking tips: Prepare the *gougères* two or three days ahead, filling them the morning of the party. Shell the beans two days before the party, then assemble the salad the day before. The morning of the party, prepare the Belgian endive appetizers, and slice the tomatoes and arrange them with the cheese. Cover them with plastic wrap and refrigerate. Later, bring them to room temperature and, just before serving, dress them with the olive oil, salt, and basil.

Also in the morning, prepare the vinaigrette in the salad bowl or bowls, and just before serving, add the greens and mix.

If possible, have two or even three grills available—one for the lamb, one for the fish, and one for the vegetables, so that all can be cooking at the same time. If not, cook the vegetables first, as these are fine served at room temperature, whereas the lamb and fish are best hot or warm from the grill.

If you are expecting a group of ten or twenty, you and your spouse or a friend can handle the grilling. If you are expecting a larger group of up to fifty, I suggest having designated grillers, so you can properly attend to your guests. I have several brothers-in-law and a close friend who love to take over the grills.

As for dessert, I suggest you order a wedding cake from your favorite fine bakery or pastry chef—one that specializes in wedding cakes and can show you photos of ones they have done. I'd also suggest that you request a tasting of the combination of cake, filling, and frosting that you choose. Ethel's was a three-tiered chocolate cake with raspberry filling and chocolate fondant frosting, decorated with fresh roses and dozens of delicately crafted dragonflies, butterflies, honeybees, even a praying mantis, made of spun sugar. Some of them were suspended over the cake, which stood on a satin-covered table beneath our 400-year-old black walnut tree. In addition, we had little tarts served to each table, but pretty sugar cookies are lovely as well for a little something extra for the guests.

belgian endive with crème fraîche and smoked salmon

This is truly one of my favorite appetizers for any time of year. Sometimes I use salmon roe instead of the smoked salmon, or smoked trout with a little lemon zest, and even, on a splurge, caviar. These appetizers are easy to eat and easy to make as well. Assemble them in the morning, then cover and refrigerate until serving time.

With the tip of a paring knife, remove the core of each Belgian endive by cutting out a cone at the base. Separate the leaves. Each head will yield about 8 large "petals." Reserve the small leaves for another use.

Mix the crème fraîche and the goat cheese together. Put a dab—about ½ to 1 teaspoon—of the mixture at the stem end of each endive petal. Remove the skin from the salmon and tear the fish into small pieces. Sprinkle each cheese dab with a little of the salmon. Arrange on a tray, cover, and refrigerate until ready to serve.

MAKES ABOUT 40 TO 48 PETALS, ENOUGH FOR 10 SERVINGS

5 to 6 heads Belgian endive
4 ounces crème fraîche
2 ounces soft, fresh goat cheese
8-ounce slab smoked salmon

*gougères filled with herbed goat cheese,
and belgian endive with crème
fraîche and smoked salmon*

gougères filled with herbed goat cheese

Gougères, *airy puffs made with the same* pâte à choux *dough as cream puffs but without the sugar, are typical French party fare. They can be stuffed with almost anything, such as a crab, shrimp, or lobster salad (see page 137), or another savory cheese. They make the perfect one-bite appetizer. They also can be made ahead and frozen—a real advantage when entertaining.*

Preheat the oven to 425°F.

Combine the water, butter, salt, white pepper, and cayenne in a saucepan over medium-high heat. Bring it to a boil, stirring. Continue to cook until the butter has melted, 3 to 4 minutes. Add the flour all at once and mix vigorously with a wooden spoon until a thick paste forms and pulls away from the sides of the pan, about 3 minutes.

Remove the pan from the heat, and with the spoon, make a well in the center of the paste. Crack 1 egg into the well and beat it into the hot mixture, either with the wooden spoon or an electric mixer. Repeat with 3 more of the eggs.

Line 2 baking sheets with silicone mats or kitchen parchment. Lightly beat the remaining egg. Using a teaspoon to shape the *gougères*, dip the spoon into a glass of cold water, then scoop up a generous teaspoon of the mixture and push it onto the baking sheet with your fingertips (wet them first for less sticking). Repeat with the rest of the mixture, dipping the spoon in the water each time to prevent sticking. When done forming the *gougères*, brush the tops with a little of the beaten egg.

Bake for 10 minutes, then reduce the heat to 350°F and bake until the *gougères* are golden brown and crunchy, another 15 minutes. If underdone, they will be mushy and uncooked inside. When done, pierce each *gougère* with a wooden skewer, then turn off the oven.

1 cup water
6 tablespoons unsalted butter
1 teaspoon salt
½ teaspoon freshly ground white pepper
Pinch cayenne
1 cup all-purpose flour
5 large eggs
Herbed Goat Cheese (recipe follows)

Leave them in the oven for 10 more minutes. Remove them from the oven and let stand for at least 30 minutes before filling.

To store the *gougères*, let them cool to room temperature and place them in a paper bag in a cool, dry place. To freeze, seal them in a plastic freezer bag. They will keep, frozen, for up to 3 months, but I suggest using them within 2 weeks for best quality. If the *gougères* have been frozen before filling, remove them from the bag, separate them, and bring them to room temperature. Heat briefly on a baking sheet in a hot 425°F oven for about 5 minutes. Let them stand for 10 minutes.

To serve the *gougères*, cut them in half crosswise, place about ½ to 1 teaspoonful of the Herbed Goat Cheese in the bottom half of each *gougère*, and replace the top. Arrange them on a serving platter and scatter the platter with the remaining chives.

MAKES ABOUT 30 GOUGÈRES, ENOUGH FOR 10 SERVINGS

herbed goat cheese

Goat cheese—thinned with milk or cream and seasoned with green herbs such as chives, dill, tarragon, or even parsley—is a quick and easy filling.

Put the cheese in a bowl and stir in enough of the cream to make a spreadable consistency. Stir in the shallots, 2 tablespoons of the chives, and the salt. Cover the bowl and refrigerate until ready to serve.

MAKES ABOUT 3½ CUPS

4 ounces soft, fresh goat cheese

2 to 3 tablespoons heavy cream or milk

2 teaspoons minced shallots

3 tablespoons snipped chives, divided

¼ teaspoon coarse sea salt or kosher sal

grilled lamb and red pepper skewers
~ or ~
grilled halibut and yellow pepper skewers

For the wedding, we wanted easy-to-handle foods for the main course, and we decided on skewers: one lamb, in the Provençal tradition, and the other fish. Salmon was a consideration, as was sea bass, but halibut is so dense and meaty, it holds together well on a skewer.

grilled lamb and red pepper skewers

Leg of lamb is a leaner cut than the shoulder, and when cubed, it makes excellent skewers to grill. Red peppers are attractive and well paired with the lamb, but green or yellow peppers can be used instead.

In a large, nonreactive bowl or pan, combine the lamb and peppers. Pour the olive oil over the top and sprinkle with the rosemary, salt, pepper, and garlic. Turn well to coat. Cover, and let the lamb marinate for 3 to 4 hours or overnight in the refrigerator. Thread the lamb onto skewers, 3 or 4 pieces per skewer, alternating with the peppers; or you can prepare the skewers before marinating the lamb and peppers.

When you are ready to cook, build a wood or charcoal fire in a grill, or preheat a gas grill. When the coals are hot or the grill reaches 400°F, oil the surface of the grill, then place the skewers on it. Grill, turning the skewers several times, until the peppers are slightly charred on the edges and the lamb is well browned on the outside and rosy pink inside, 10 to 15 minutes total. Transfer the skewers to a platter and cover loosely with foil until ready to serve.

MAKES ABOUT 16 SKEWERS, ENOUGH FOR 10 SERVINGS

3 pounds boneless leg of lamb, trimmed and cut into 1½-inch cubes

4 large red bell peppers, stemmed, seeded, and cut into 1-inch squares

3 tablespoons extra-virgin olive oil

2 tablespoons finely minced fresh rosemary

2 teaspoons coarse sea salt or kosher salt

1 teaspoon freshly ground black pepper

4 cloves crushed garlic

grilled halibut and yellow pepper skewers,
and fresh shelling and green bean
salad with winter savory

grilled halibut and yellow pepper skewers

Halibut is an excellent choice for grilling on skewers because of its firm texture and rich flavor. We chose to pair the fish with yellow peppers because we felt their milder flavor was a better accompaniment than red peppers.

In a large, nonreactive bowl or pan, combine the halibut and peppers. Pour the olive oil over the top and sprinkle with the salt, pepper, thyme, and lemon zest. Cover, and let the halibut marinate for 30 minutes. Prepare the skewers, threading 3 or 4 pieces of fish per skewer, alternating with the peppers; or you can prepare the skewers before marinating the halibut and peppers.

If using the same grill as you used for the lamb, scrub it clean with a wire brush and oil it again. Otherwise, build a wood or charcoal fire in a grill, or preheat a gas grill. When the coals are hot or the grill reaches 400°F, oil the surface of the grill, then place the skewers on it. Grill, turning the skewers once or twice, until the halibut is just opaque and the peppers are lightly charred, about 10 minutes total. Transfer the skewers to a platter and cover loosely with foil until ready to serve.

MAKES ABOUT 16 SKEWERS, ENOUGH FOR 10 SERVINGS

2½ pounds halibut fillets, about 1 inch thick, cut into 1-inch cubes
4 large yellow bell peppers, stemmed, seeded, and cut into 1-inch squares
3 tablespoons extra-virgin olive oil
½ teaspoon coarse sea salt or kosher salt
½ teaspoon freshly ground black pepper
2 tablespoons minced fresh thyme leaves
Grated zest of 2 lemons (about 4 teaspoons)

mixed grilled summer vegetables

Because there were a number of vegetarians attending Ethel's wedding, we wanted to make sure we offered them abundant options. It was a good thing we made lots of grilled vegetables, because they were in high demand by everyone.

Remove the caps from the eggplants, then cut them lengthwise into slices about ⅜ inch thick. Do the same with the zucchini. Cut the peppers in half lengthwise and remove the core and seeds. You can leave on the stem end, if desired. If the peppers are large, quarter them. If not, leave them in halves. Peel the onions and cut them crosswise into slices about ⅓ inch thick.

Put the eggplant, zucchini, and peppers together in a large bowl or baking dish. Drizzle them with the ¼ cup of olive oil, and sprinkle with the rosemary, thyme, oregano, salt, and pepper. Turn well to marinate, adding more olive oil if needed. Gently add the onion slices, keeping them intact if possible.

Turn the vegetables occasionally. You can marinate them the night before and grill them the next day, or grill them within the hour, as desired.

Build a wood or charcoal fire in a grill, or preheat a gas grill. When the coals are hot or the grill reaches 400°F, wipe the grill with olive oil. Put the remaining olive oil in a bowl and add the crushed garlic. Position it near the grill with the rosemary brush.

Arrange the eggplant, zucchini, and peppers on the grill, and let them cook, turning them and basting with the rosemary brush dipped in olive oil. Put the onions in a grilling basket, and turn and baste them as well.

3 globe or 7 Asian eggplants, about 2½ pounds

4 or 5 medium-size zucchini

6 or 7 medium-size red bell peppers

3 large yellow onions

¼ to ⅓ cup extra-virgin olive oil, plus ½ cup for basting

2 tablespoons minced fresh rosemary

2 tablespoons minced fresh thyme leaves

2 tablespoons minced fresh oregano or marjoram leaves

1 teaspoon coarse sea salt or kosher salt

1 teaspoon freshly ground black pepper

6 cloves garlic, crushed

6 to 8 branches fresh rosemary tied with kitchen string to use as basting brush

The zucchini is ready when it is golden brown, about 3 to 4 minutes per side. The eggplant is done when it has a golden-brown crust on both sides, about 5 minutes per side. The peppers are ready when they are soft and lightly charred, about 5 minutes per side. When the onions are translucent and turning golden brown on the edges, they are ready, about 10 to 15 minutes total.

Remove the grilled vegetables to a serving platter, arranging them by type or mixing them, as you prefer. Cover loosely with foil and set them aside until you are ready to serve. Serve the vegetables warm or at room temperature.

MAKES 10 SERVINGS

heirloom tomato platter with purple basil

It wouldn't be a summer feast without a platter of heirloom tomatoes, and Ethel's wedding was no exception. A neighboring organic farmer and his wife gave flats of their heirloom tomatoes as a wedding gift, delivering them to the catering company the day before the wedding.

Core and slice the heirloom tomatoes and arrange them on a serving platter. Halve the cherry tomatoes and scatter these across the top. Sprinkle the tomatoes with the salt and half the basil. Drizzle them with the olive oil and top with the remaining basil.

Serve at room temperature.

MAKES 10 SERVINGS

10 large or 20 medium-size heirloom tomatoes, or a combination, of various colors and varieties

1 pint mixed cherry tomato varieties (optional)

1½ teaspoons coarse sea salt or kosher salt

1 cup fresh purple basil leaves, torn, small leaves left whole

2 to 3 tablespoons extra-virgin olive oil

heirloom tomato platter with purple basil

fresh shelling and green bean salad with winter savory

This scrumptious salad was tricky because the shelling bean season had just started, but we managed to find enough fresh cranberry beans to make it. In the garden I had the winter savory, which is a very good flavoring for beans, as well as the basil. If you can't find fresh shelling beans, purchase dried ones and cook one cup according to the directions. Drain and use them in the salad in lieu of the fresh shelling beans.

TO PREPARE THE BEANS

Combine the water, ½ teaspoon of the salt, and 3 of the winter savory sprigs in a large saucepan or pot over medium-high heat, and bring them to a boil. Add the shelling beans and cook for 8 to 10 minutes, until just tender. Do not overcook. Let them stand in the cooking water to cool. Remove the beans with a strainer, reserving the cooking liquid in the pot, and set the beans aside.

Turn the heat to medium-high, add the remaining salt and savory sprigs, and bring to a boil again. Add the haricots verts and cook until tender and no longer crunchy, 3 to 7 minutes. Transfer them to a colander, rinse under cold running water, drain, and set aside.

TO PREPARE THE MARINADE

Put the salt and garlic in a bowl or mortar. Using the back of a fork or a pestle, crush them together into a paste. With a fork, incorporate the olive oil, and then the lemon juice and pepper.

Put the mixture in a large bowl and add the shelling beans, haricots verts, and basil. Turn well to coat, then cover and refrigerate overnight. Marinating the beans will dilute the marinade, so before serving, the seasonings must be adjusted.

BEANS

8 cups water

¾ teaspoon coarse sea salt or kosher salt, divided

6 sprigs fresh winter savory or thyme

3 pounds fresh cranberry beans, cannellini beans, black-eyed peas, or a mix of these or other fresh shelling beans, shelled

3 pounds thin, tender haricots verts, trimmed, or substitute Blue Lake or other young, tender green beans

MARINADE

½ teaspoon coarse sea salt or kosher salt

2 cloves garlic

½ cup extra-virgin olive oil

4 to 5 tablespoons (about 2 lemons) freshly squeezed lemon juice

½ teaspoon freshly ground black pepper

½ cup julienned fresh basil leaves

TO SERVE

When you are ready to serve, first taste the beans, then add additional lemon juice, salt, pepper, and basil until they are well-seasoned: the beans should not be bland. Add about half the curls of Parmesan cheese and turn well.

Place the beans in a serving bowl or arrange them on a platter and top with the remaining Parmesan cheese curls.

MAKES 10 SERVINGS

SERVING

2 to 3 tablespoons (about 1 lemon) freshly squeezed lemon juice

½ teaspoon coarse sea salt or kosher salt

½ teaspoon freshly ground black pepper

⅓ cup julienned fresh basil leaves or whole baby basil leaves

3 ounces Parmesan cheese, shaved into curls with a vegetable peeler

salad of mixed greens

Where we live it is too hot in July to grow lettuce, so for Ethel's wedding I ordered 40 pounds of mixed baby field greens from a farmer friend near Salinas, California, where the moderate coastal climate allows for near year-round production. He delivered the fresh baby greens himself, the night before the wedding.

Combine the shallots, olive oil, mustard, and salt in a large salad bowl, and with a fork or whisk, mix until a thick emulsion forms, about 2 minutes. Add the vinegar and mix until well blended, then set aside until ready to serve. Just before serving, add the greens to the bowl and mix together gently with the dressing.

MAKES 10 SERVINGS

¼ cup minced shallots
½ cup extra-virgin olive oil
1 tablespoon Dijon mustard
1½ to 2 teaspoons coarse sea salt
   or kosher salt
¼ cup red wine vinegar
15 cups mixed young, tender
   salad greens

frosted sugar cookies

These can be served before the wedding cake, as a little something sweet to nibble on while waiting for the big moment of cutting the cake and toasting to the happy couple. Cut the cookies into rounds, stars, half moons, or whatever fits the overall theme of your wedding party, and decorate them with frosting that reflects the day's color scheme.

Preheat the oven to 400°F.

Using a food processor, pulse the butter and sugar together until fluffy, about 2 minutes. Add the egg and pulse several times to blend.

Whisk together the flour, baking powder, and salt in a bowl. Add the flour mixture to the butter mixture in 3 portions, pulsing briefly after each addition, until the flour is absorbed and a soft ball of dough forms, about 2 minutes total.

On a lightly floured board, roll out the dough to a thickness of about ⅛ inch. Using cookie cutters or templates, cut the dough into the desired shapes and arrange them 1½ inches apart on ungreased baking sheets.

Gather up the scraps and form them lightly into a ball. Roll out the dough as before, and continue cutting cookies until you have used up all of the dough.

Bake until the cookies are just lightly browned on the bottom and pale golden on top, 6 to 8 minutes.

Remove from the oven and let the cookies cool on the baking sheets for 5 minutes. With a spatula, transfer the cookies to a work surface. Thinly spread the cookies with Royal Icing. Let the icing dry completely before serving or storing the cookies.

MAKES ABOUT TWENTY-FIVE 2-INCH COOKIES

⅔ cup unsalted butter, at room temperature
½ cup sugar
1 egg
1¾ cups flour
½ teaspoon baking powder
¼ teaspoon fine sea salt
Royal Icing (page 121)

summer solstice

GRILLED PAIN AU LEVAIN WITH WALNUT TAPENADE

PALMIERS À LA NIÇOISE

GRILLED BONELESS LEG OF LAMB WITH ROSEMARY AND ROMESCO SAUCE

NEW POTATO AND ARUGULA SALAD WITH BLACK OLIVES

GOLDEN BEET AND FRESH MOZZARELLA SALAD

GRILLED PEACHES WITH WHIPPED CREAM AND BLUEBERRIES

the party

A number of my friends in Provence use the summer solstice, or Feast of St. John, as an excuse to have a party and welcome the season. The menu ranges from wild boar and stuffed whole lamb to grilled lamb chops or simply a mix of sausages, with lots of salads, vegetables, and a seasonal fruit dessert. *Pastis*, the anise-flavored aperitif native to Provence, and wine are poured liberally, and platters of tapenade toasts and bowls of olives are passed among the convivial crowd. At 10 p.m., when it is time to sit down to dinner, the sky is still lavender with the waning light.

The traditional bonfire of local olive and juniper wood is stacked waist high, ready to be lit at midnight, and then follows much fanfare and dancing. In the old days, the village boys would jump over the fire while the admiring girls watched. Last summer I was unable to be in Provence, so I decided to have a summer solstice celebration in California, raising a glass of my husband's rosé to our friends in the Old World, toasting together the long days of summer.

I chose to keep things simple, filling the dishes with the tastes of Provence—olives, tomatoes, and herbs. I eschewed my natural inclination to dramatically roast a whole beast and instead offered grilled boneless leg of lamb—equally good and far less work. To serve with the lamb, a luscious *romesco* sauce. Grilled *pain au levain* with a spread, a savory puff pastry filled with the flavors of Provence, and olives comprised the appetizers. Tender early-summer golden beets, sliced and topped with fresh mozzarella and purple basil just clipped from the gardens composed one salad, and freshly dug new potatoes with young arugula the other. The dessert, a departure from my usual fruit tart, was grilled peaches with whipped cream and blueberries, which tastes like a warm cobbler or tart without the crust. We did forgo the bonfire. It had been a dry spring, and it seemed a little too risky to have one; maybe next time.

Decorating tips: Arrange masses of early-summer flowers, such as sweet peas, zinnias, and roses mixed with greens in low bowls on the table; include lots of candles and lanterns if the party is outside, and streamers of ribbons, in the same shades as the flowers, tacked to tall poles set around the table. These will wave in the wind and create a festive atmosphere.

Cooking tips: As they enjoy their drinks, the guests can grill their own bread slices and spread them, hot off the grill, with the tapenade. Instead of the boneless leg of lamb, you could certainly substitute pork chops or sausages. For a larger group, you could also offer flageolet beans, the traditional accompaniment to leg of lamb.

grilled pain au levain with walnut tapenade

There are dozens of versions of tapenade, which is basically a seasoned olive spread, and this one uses walnuts, of which I have a year-round supply from my walnut-farming neighbors, plus dried tomatoes, which give the spread some tang. The spread can be made a day ahead and refrigerated.

Place the olives in a blender or food processor with the walnuts, tomatoes, tomato oil, and thyme. Blend or process until the mixture is well mixed. Slowly add olive oil, puréeing or processing until the mixture reaches the desired consistency for spreading.

Grill the toasts as your guests arrive, which is fun, or you can grill them in advance.

MAKES 1 CUP TAPENADE AND 30 APPETIZERS, ENOUGH FOR 6 TO 8 SERVINGS

⅓ cup oil-cured black olives, pitted and coarsely chopped
⅓ cup walnuts, coarsely chopped
¼ cup oil-packed dried tomatoes, coarsely chopped
½ teaspoon oil reserved from the dried tomatoes
1 teaspoon fresh thyme leaves
2 to 4 tablespoons extra-virgin olive oil
10 to 15 thin slices *pain au levain*, cut in half to make toasts about 2 by 3 inches

palmiers à la niçoise

This is a savory version of the classic French cookie, perfect for aperitif time. I especially like to serve these before the meal with a glass of pastis, *the iconic licorice-flavored drink favored in Provence—I can close my eyes and imagine that I'm in the south of France. The palmiers can be prepared ahead, then covered and refrigerated for up to six hours before slicing and baking. You can also divide the pastry dough in half and make individual rolls.*

Preheat the oven to 425°F.

Heat the olive oil in a frying pan over medium-high heat. When the oil is hot, add the onions and reduce the heat to medium-low. Cook, stirring often, until the onions are limp and soft, but not browned, about 7 minutes. Stir in the pepper and tomatoes; cook for 1 minute more. Season with a little salt and pepper to taste.

Remove the pan from the heat and stir in the olives and thyme.

On a lightly floured work surface, roll out the puff pastry to a scant ¼ inch thickness. Place it on a sheet of plastic wrap. Cover the surface with a thin coating of the onion mixture, spreading it all the way to the edges. Roll each of the long sides inward, toward the center, keeping them snug. You will have 2 connected rolls, meeting in the center—think of a pair of eyeglasses. With a pastry brush or your fingertips, dampen the inner roll with water and press together. Wrap the completed roll with the plastic wrap and refrigerate for 20 minutes. Remove and cut the roll into slices a generous ¼ inch thick.

2½ teaspoons extra-virgin olive oil
½ pound onions, finely chopped
½ red pepper, seeded and minced
¼ cup dried tomatoes packed in olive oil, minced
Coarse sea salt or kosher salt
Freshly ground black pepper
¼ cup oil-cured black olives, pitted, minced
½ teaspoon minced fresh thyme leaves
1 sheet frozen puff pastry, thawed according to package directions

Sprinkle a little water on 2 nonstick baking sheets, and place the slices flat on the sheets, leaving about 1 inch between each slice.

Chill the baking sheets in the freezer for 10 minutes, then bake the *palmiers* until puffed and golden, about 15 to 20 minutes. Remove from the oven and let the *palmiers* cool slightly. Serve warm.

MAKES ABOUT 30 APPETIZERS, ENOUGH FOR 6 TO 8 SERVINGS

grilled boneless leg of lamb with rosemary and romesco sauce

Lamb in many forms has a perennial place at Provençal meals because sheep are indigenous to the area, where they feed on the wild herbs and shrubs that flavor the meat. Herbes de Provence—a dried mixture of winter savory, thyme, rosemary, and a sprinkling of other herbs—is the typical seasoning, but here I decided to use only rosemary, which flourishes along my garden walkway, and to serve the lamb with a flavorful romesco sauce.

Build a wood or charcoal fire in a grill, or preheat a gas grill.

Trim most of the fat from the lamb, and rub the lamb all over with the olive oil. In a small bowl, mix together the salt, pepper, and rosemary and rub it on the meat. Make 1-inch-deep slits all over the meat, about 20 altogether, and slip the slivers of garlic deep into the slits.

When the coals are hot or the grill reaches 400°F, put the meat on. Turn it often and cook until an instant-read thermometer inserted into the thickest part reads 135°F to 140°F.

Transfer the meat to a cutting board, cover, and let it stand for 15 minutes before carving it into thin slices. To serve, arrange the slices on a warmed platter, drizzle with any reserved juices, and garnish with the rosemary sprigs. Serve the Romesco Sauce along with the meat.

MAKES 8 TO 10 SERVINGS

3½- to 4-pound butterflied boneless leg of lamb (have your butcher butterfly the lamb for you)

2 tablespoons extra-virgin olive oil

2 teaspoons coarse sea salt or kosher salt

2 teaspoons freshly ground black pepper

2 tablespoons minced fresh rosemary, plus several sprigs for garnish

4 cloves garlic, cut lengthwise into thin slivers

Romesco Sauce (recipe follows)

romesco sauce

An Italian specialty of roasted tomatoes and peppers, romesco sauce is often used in Provence to accompany meat and fish. Like the tapenade, you can make it a day ahead and keep it covered in the refrigerator. Bring the sauce to room temperature before serving.

Preheat the oven to 400°F.

Arrange the tomato halves cut side down in a pan just large enough to hold them along with the pepper and the garlic. Roast until the pepper is tender and its skin slips off easily, and the tomatoes have released some of their juices and their skins slip off, about 35 minutes.

Remove the pan from the oven, and when the pepper is cool enough to handle, peel and discard the skin, cut it in half, and remove the seeds and core. Chop the pepper into 3 or 4 pieces. Remove and discard the tomato skins. Squeeze the garlic, releasing the roasted pulp, and discard the skins.

Put the roasted tomatoes, pepper, garlic, almonds, bread, salt, and red pepper flakes in a blender and process until a thick paste forms. Slowly add enough of the olive oil to achieve a creamy consistency. Set the sauce aside until ready to serve.

MAKES ABOUT 1½ CUPS SAUCE, ENOUGH FOR 8 TO 10 SERVINGS

2 ripe, juicy tomatoes, halved
1 large red bell pepper, whole
4 cloves garlic, unpeeled
⅓ cup (about 1¾ ounces) almonds
1 slice *pain au levain* or other rustic coarse-crumbed bread, torn into pieces
½ teaspoon salt
¼ to ½ teaspoon crushed red pepper flakes
2 to 3 tablespoons extra-virgin olive oil

new potato and arugula salad
with black olives

This is a light, French-style version of potato salad, showcasing the sweet flavor of new potatoes. I used Yukon Golds, the variety we had growing in our garden, but others, such as German Butterballs, fingerlings, and even small red potatoes, could be used as well. The potatoes are best dressed a few hours before serving to let the flavors meld; add the remaining arugula at the last minute so it is crisp when the salad is served.

Put the potatoes in a large saucepan, cover them with 2 inches of water, and bring them to a boil over high heat. Reduce the heat to low, cover, and simmer until the potatoes are just barely tender when pierced with a fork, about 20 minutes. Do not overcook.

Drain the potatoes, and when cool enough to handle but while still warm, cut them into ½-inch slices. Put the slices in a bowl, add 2 tablespoons of the olive oil, the vinegar, salt, and pepper. Gently turn to coat. Add half the arugula and gently turn again.

Arrange the remaining arugula on a serving platter or individual plates and top with the potato mixture, then garnish with the olives. If desired, drizzle with the remaining olive oil.

MAKES 8 TO 10 SERVINGS

10 to 12 (about 1½ pounds) small to medium-size new potatoes
¼ cup extra-virgin olive oil
1 tablespoon white wine vinegar or Champagne vinegar
½ teaspoon coarse sea salt or kosher salt
½ teaspoon freshly ground black pepper
2½ cups baby arugula
¼ cup whole or pitted oil-cured black olives

golden beet and fresh mozzarella salad

This combination of gold and white complements the other colors in the meal, making for a bright presentation worthy of a summer solstice celebration. I prefer to boil rather than roast the beets because golden beets often turn brown when roasted—tasty, but not as pretty. You can use red beets, of course, but they will color whatever they touch a pinkish red. Using purple basil can be especially striking with golden beets. Later in the summer, when the tomatoes are ripe, I alternate layers of beets and tomatoes with the cheese.

Put the beets in a large pot, cover with water by 2 inches, and bring to a boil over high heat. Cover and reduce the heat to medium. Cook the beets until they are tender enough to be pierced easily by a fork, 45 minutes to 1 hour. Drain the beets, and when they are cool enough to handle, peel them and cut into thin slices. Set the beets aside.

Cut the mozzarella into generous ¼-inch-thick slices, then cut the slices in half. If using the very small balls of mozzarella (*bocconcini*), simply cut them in half.

Arrange the beet and mozzarella slices on a platter, alternating them to make a pattern. Tuck basil leaves in randomly or in a pattern. Drizzle with the olive oil and sprinkle with salt to taste.

MAKES 8 TO 10 SERVINGS

3 or 4 medium-size golden beets, about 1½ pounds

8 to 10 ounces fresh mozzarella cheese

12 to 15 large fresh basil leaves, more if small

3 to 4 tablespoons extra-virgin olive oil

Coarse sea salt or kosher salt

*grilled peaches with whipped cream
and blueberries*

grilled peaches with whipped cream and blueberries

Grilling the peaches caramelizes them slightly, bringing out all their sweetness. The cream and blueberries are an added attraction. Since peaches are often sold when mature but not yet soft or ripe, plan to buy your peaches a few days early and set them out in your kitchen to ripen.

Heat a pot of water over high heat. When it is boiling, gently slide the peaches into the water, removing them after 20 seconds or so. When they are cool enough to handle, slip off the skins, cut them in half, and remove the pits. Set the peaches aside.

Whip the cream with an electric mixer until stiff peaks form, 3 to 4 minutes. Beat in the sugar, and set the whipped cream aside.

Build a wood or charcoal fire in a grill, or preheat a gas grill. When the coals are hot or the grill reaches 400°F, rub it with some of the olive oil.

Rub the peaches gently on both sides with olive oil. Place them cut side down on the grill and cook just long enough to sear, about 2 minutes. Turn and sear the other side, about 2 minutes. Remove them to a platter or individual serving plates. Top the peaches with the whipped cream and sprinkle with the blueberries.

MAKES 8 TO 10 SERVINGS

10 ripe peaches
1½ cups heavy cream
2 tablespoons sugar
About 4 tablespoons extra-virgin olive oil
2 cups blueberries

movie night

SALUMI AND ANTIPASTI PLATTER

GRATINÉED CRESPELLE WITH MUSHROOM AND SPINACH FILLING

RED AND YELLOW CHERRY TOMATO SALAD

FRESH NECTARINE TIRAMISU

salumi and antipasti platter

the party

Getting together with friends to watch a movie and share a meal that corresponds to its theme or nationality makes for a good party anytime of year. If the movie is an old favorite that we've already seen, I'll serve the food along with the movie, and everyone makes comments and reminisces while the images flicker. If it's a new film, or one that we need to pay close attention to, I'll serve only the appetizers with the movie, and the main course and dessert follow while we talk about the film. When possible, it's a lot of fun to watch the movie and eat outside, accompanied by the night sounds of summer and lit by shafts of moonlight.

Here I've put together a menu to go with an Italian movie, perhaps the 1960 Fellini classic, *La Dolce Vita*.

Decorating tips: Old movie posters, an old-fashioned movie projector, film reels, vintage film magazines—things you might have found at a flea market and bought just for fun—this is an opportunity to make good use of them. Add a bouquet or two of bright summer flowers, and you are all set.

Cooking tips: For a shortcut, buy cannoli, a fancy meringue, or other dessert from a favorite bakery instead of making the tiramisu. For a larger meal, in case of a long movie or a movie marathon, treat the *crespelle* as a first course and follow with a meat dish and vegetable, such as roast pork and potatoes. You can serve the salad before, with, or after the *crespelle*.

salumi and antipasti platter

There are so many excellent artisanal cured meats and Italian-style vegetables available now that it is easy to put together an antipasti platter that will make your guests feel as if they are in Italy. The key is to mix several different flavors, textures, and colors. Serve the platter with purchased breadsticks or toasted bread.

Attractively arrange the meats and cheese on a serving platter. Drain the peperoncini and olives, reserving their brines for storing any leftovers, and add them to the platter.

MAKES 8 SERVINGS

½ to ¾ pound selected cured meats such as *sopressata*, prosciutto, *mortadella*, or others, thinly sliced

½ pound thinly sliced provolone cheese

8 ounces pickled peperoncini or red cherry peppers, or a mixture

8 ounces mixed olives

gratinéed crespelle with mushroom and spinach filling

Crespelle are the Italian version of the French crepe, but the batter is slightly lighter than its French counterpart. The thin pancakes can be made the day before, wrapped in plastic wrap, and refrigerated until the next day. You can prepare the filling the day before as well. On the day of the party, prepare the cheese sauce, then assemble the dish and keep it refrigerated, for up to four hours, until you are ready to bake.

You can serve them with just about any filling you like, but I usually keep it simple, favoring greens. The recipe may seem complicated at first, but if you organize your ingredients before getting started, you'll find that it's really quite simple.

TO PREPARE THE CRESPELLE

Pour the milk into a mixing bowl, and very slowly whisk in the flour, being careful not to let lumps form. Stir in the salt, and then the eggs, whisking well until a thin batter forms.

In an 8-inch nonstick frying pan, melt 1 teaspoon of the butter over medium-high heat. When it foams, pour 2 tablespoons of the batter (I use a ¼-cup measure, filling it only halfway) into the pan, quickly tilting and swirling the pan to cover the bottom with a thin layer of batter. After about a minute, the edges of the *crespella* will begin to curl and bubbles will form on the surface, indicating that the bottom of the pancake is browning. Turn carefully and cook the other side until pale golden, another few seconds. Remove the *crespella* to a plate, and repeat, using just enough butter for each one to prevent it from sticking to the pan, until all the batter has been used. You should have 17 or 18 *crespelle*.

CRESPELLE

1 cup whole milk
¾ cup all-purpose flour
Pinch fine sea salt or table salt
2 eggs
2 tablespoons unsalted butter, divided

MUSHROOM AND SPINACH FILLING

1½ teaspoons coarse sea salt or kosher salt, divided
1 pound fresh spinach, well washed, drained, any tough stems removed
½ pound any variety fresh mushrooms
1 tablespoon unsalted butter
2 tablespoons minced shallots
½ teaspoon freshly ground black pepper
2 tablespoons minced fresh flat-leaf parsley

TO PREPARE THE FILLING

Bring a large pot of water to a boil over high heat. Add 1 teaspoon of the salt, and then add the spinach. Reduce the heat to medium-high and cook just until the spinach is limp but still bright green, 3 to 4 minutes. Remove and drain the spinach, rinse it under cold water, and squeeze it dry. Chop the spinach and squeeze it dry again. It is important to ensure that the filling is not watery. Set the spinach aside.

Trim off any tough or discolored mushroom stem ends and discard. Mince the mushrooms, including the stems.

Heat the butter in a frying pan over medium-high heat. When it foams, add the shallots and sauté until translucent, 2 to 3 minutes. Add the mushrooms and sauté until they are soft and have released their juices, 4 to 5 minutes. Add the chopped spinach and the remaining salt, the pepper, and parsley. Continue to cook until the liquid has evaporated, another few minutes. Transfer the vegetables to a bowl and set them aside.

TO PREPARE THE SAUCE

Melt the butter in a saucepan over medium-high heat. When it has melted, remove it from the heat and whisk in the flour to make a roux, or paste. Return the pan to the heat and slowly drizzle in the milk, whisking it in thoroughly to prevent any lumping. Add the salt, pepper, and cayenne and reduce the heat to medium. Continue to whisk from time to time, until the sauce has thickened. Add the Parmesan to the sauce and mix. Spoon about ½ cup of the sauce into the mushroom and spinach filling, and stir until the mixture is sticky, but not runny. Add more sauce if necessary.

CHEESE SAUCE

2½ tablespoons unsalted butter
2 tablespoons all-purpose flour
1¾ cups whole milk
½ teaspoon coarse sea salt or kosher salt
½ teaspoon freshly ground black pepper
¼ teaspoon cayenne
⅔ cup freshly grated Parmesan cheese

FINISHING THE GRATIN

½ teaspoon plus ½ tablespoon unsalted butter
⅓ cup freshly grated Parmesan cheese

TO FINISH THE DISH

Preheat the oven to 450°F.

Butter a gratin dish or baking dish with the ½ teaspoon of butter. Take a *crespella* and lay it on a work surface. Place about 1 tablespoon of the filling down the center, spreading it no closer than 1 inch to the edge. Roll it up and place it seam side down in the baking dish. Repeat until all the *crespelle* are filled and snugly tucked into the dish. Pour the cheese sauce over the *crespelle*, dot with the remaining butter, and sprinkle with the Parmesan cheese.

If you are working with *crespelle* and filling that have been refrigerated, bake the gratin for 15 to 20 minutes. If your ingredients were still warm, bake for about 10 minutes. In either case, at the end of the baking time, place the gratin under a hot broiler for 3 to 5 minutes for a crispy topping.

Remove the gratin and let it stand for about 5 minutes before serving. To serve, slip a spatula under the *crespelle*, 1 or 2 at a time, and arrange on a dinner plate.

MAKES 8 SERVINGS

red and yellow cherry tomato salad

My summer garden is always overrun with cherry tomatoes, because each spring I unfailingly overplant, forgetting that cherry tomatoes are among the most productive tomatoes of all, and that come summer, their thick foliage and heavy burden of fruit will spill over their stakes and strings. However, besides being luscious right off the vine, they make exceptional but simple summer salads, like this one. The salad, made an hour ahead, allows the tomatoes to steep in the vinaigrette and lend their juices to it. The greens are added at the last minute.

Cut the tomatoes in half, placing them in a bowl as you cut them. This helps reserve the juices.

Combine the oil, vinegar, salt, and pepper in a salad bowl. Add the tomatoes. Just before serving, add the greens and toss well.

MAKES 8 SERVINGS

4 cups mixed cherry tomatoes, stems removed
3 tablespoons extra-virgin olive oil
1 tablespoon red wine vinegar
¼ teaspoon coarse sea salt or kosher salt
¼ teaspoon freshly ground black pepper
4 cups mixed young lettuces or greens

fresh nectarine tiramisu

This is a decadent, rich dessert, just right to accompany an Italian movie—or to enjoy anytime. The nectarines turn the classic tiramisu into a celebration of summer. The sweet, juicy fruit sits atop the ladyfingers, mingling their flavor with the hazelnut liqueur in which the ladyfingers have been soaked.

3 egg yolks

4 tablespoons sugar

1 to 1⅓ cups Frangelico (hazelnut liqueur), divided

8 ounces mascarpone cheese, at room temperature

¼ cup brewed espresso

2 egg whites

½ cup heavy cream

4 to 5 ripe medium-size nectarines, 1½ to 2 pounds

12 to 14 (about 3 ounces) packaged ladyfinger cookies

Combine the egg yolks and sugar in the top section of a double boiler, and place it over, but not touching, gently simmering water. Beat the mixture with a whisk or electric mixer until it turns pale yellow and thick ribbons form when dropped from a spoon, about 5 minutes. Add 3 tablespoons of the Frangelico and continue to whisk or beat until once again the mixture forms thick ribbons.

Combine the mascarpone and the espresso in a small bowl, blending well.

Beat the egg whites with an electric mixer until stiff peaks form, then gently fold them into the egg yolk mixture.

Wash the beater and then beat the heavy cream until soft peaks form.

Pit and cut 3 or 4 of the nectarines into ½-inch-thick slices. Reserve 1 whole nectarine for the garnish.

Separate the ladyfingers into halves. Dip each half, one by one, into the remaining Frangelico, and arrange them in an 8-inch trifle bowl or a 9-inch square dish that is at least 2 inches deep.

Arrange a layer of sliced nectarines on top of the ladyfingers. Gently spread with a layer of the mascarpone, then a layer of the egg yolk mixture, then a layer of whipped cream. Repeat the layers, starting with soaking the remaining ladyfingers, piece by piece, in the Frangelico.

When done, cover the dish with plastic wrap and refrigerate for 4 to 5 hours, or up to 12 hours, before serving. Just before serving, slice the remaining nectarine and arrange the slices on top of the tiramisu. To serve, scoop out portions with a large serving spoon or spatula.

MAKES 8 TO 10 SERVINGS

a housewarming

✳

HEIRLOOM TOMATO BLOODY MARYS

CRISPY WONTON SQUARES TOPPED WITH SPICY AHI TUNA

GARLIC-GRILLED SHRIMP

OVEN-ROASTED NECTARINES WITH CREMA AND TOASTED PISTACHIOS

heirloom tomato bloody marys

the party

Although I've lived in my current home in Northern California for more than 20 years, every summer I like to celebrate the house that is my home, and the bounty that its gardens provide me and my extended family and friends—a sort of annual housewarming, as I think of it.

The party is held in the backyard, with its grape arbor and old black walnut tree, the lawns and granite spaces hedged with rosemary and sweet bay laurel. I keep the food simple but special, serving it in courses rather than all at once or buffet style. The tables and chairs are scattered in groups where everyone can sit comfortably, instead of at a formal table. The shrimp are grilled whole, and hungry guests peel and discard the shells, so I have bowls on hand for the carcasses, as well as plenty of napkins. It's a congenial and relaxed party, with everyone peeling shrimp, and laughing and talking over the food and wine.

As the sky turns mauve at the coming of dusk, we'll be just finishing up our dessert.

Decorating tips: Bowls of tomatoes, peaches, and nectarines with sprigs of rosemary tucked alongside them make fragrant and beautiful accents, and you can send them home with your guests at the end of the party.

Cooking tips: Have pitchers of the different tomato juices made up before guests arrive, with backup pitchers on hand in the refrigerator. If you want extra appetizers, serve some olives, nuts, and maybe a bowl of cherry tomatoes. For a more substantial meal, roast and thinly slice a beef tenderloin, and add a green salad. This meal could also be served buffet style, with only the drinks and the crispy wontons with ahi as appetizers.

heirloom tomato bloody marys

I think this is one of the most spectacular drinks, and one that can be enjoyed only in that slice of time when the deeply flavored heirloom tomatoes, such as Cherokee Purple, Red Brandywine, Marvel Stripe, Persimmon, Golden Jubilee, Evergreen, Green Grape, and Green Zebra, are at the height of summer sweetness.

The tomato juice will be frothy after being puréed and will not look like "regular" tomato juice, but what a taste! I make three pitchers—one using yellow tomatoes, one with red, and one with green—and while similar, each has not only its own color but also its particular flavor. I've found that guests want to sample them all, so I serve smaller-than-traditional pours.

You may want to add all of the Bloody Mary mix to the pitchers of juice before your guests arrive, but this will slightly darken the color of the yellow and green tomato juices.

TO PREPARE THE GARNISHES

Use a vegetable peeler or paring knife to remove 9 long, thin strips of cucumber peel. Cut 9 thin slices of cucumber lengthwise. To assemble, wrap a strip of cucumber peel around a cucumber slice, a celery rib, and a red pepper slice to make a bundle, and fasten with a toothpick. Repeat, making 8 more vegetable bundles, and set them aside.

TO PREPARE THE TOMATO JUICES

Using a blender, purée the red tomatoes with ¼ cup of the chopped onion, and pour the juice into a small pitcher. Repeat with the yellow and the green tomatoes, to make 3 separate pitchers of red, yellow, and green tomato juice.

VEGETABLE GARNISH BUNDLES

1 large cucumber, preferably unwaxed
9 small celery ribs, leaves attached
9 thin slices red bell pepper

TOMATO JUICES

3 cups chopped red tomatoes
¾ cup chopped onion, divided
3 cups chopped yellow or orange tomatoes
3 cups chopped green tomatoes

BLOODY MARY MIX

Juice of 1½ lemons (about 4 tablespoons)
Juice of 1½ limes (about 3 tablespoons)
6 teaspoons Tabasco sauce
3 heaping teaspoons prepared horseradish
1½ teaspoons celery salt
1½ teaspoons freshly ground black pepper
1 teaspoon sweet or mild paprika

TO PREPARE THE BLOODY MARY MIX

In a measuring cup, combine the lemon juice, lime juice, Tabasco sauce, horseradish, celery salt, black pepper, and paprika. Mix well, then pour about one-third of the mix into each pitcher and stir.

TO SERVE

Put several ice cubes in an 8-ounce glass and pour about 1½ ounces of vodka over them, followed with about 5 ounces of red, yellow, or green tomato juice. Stir and garnish each glass with a vegetable bundle.

MAKES NINE 6½-OUNCE COCKTAILS

SERVING

Ice
14 ounces vodka

*crispy wonton squares topped
with spicy ahi tuna*

crispy wonton squares topped with spicy ahi tuna

Instead of the usual crackers, crispy wontons, fried earlier in the day, make the base for a spicy raw ahi tuna topping, which pairs deliciously with the Bloody Marys. The spice comes from harissa *paste, a flavorful North African blend of peppers, tomatoes, and spices, which is available at many Middle Eastern markets, specialty shops, or online.*

Choose top-grade ahi tuna, and you won't be disappointed. If you are reluctant to serve raw fish, you could sear the ahi before dicing it.

Cut the tuna into ¼-inch dice and set aside.

In a large bowl, mix together the mayonnaise, lime juice, salt, and *harissa*. Cover and refrigerate until you are ready to serve.

Cut each of the wonton wrappers into approximately 4 equal squares. Heat 2 inches of oil in a Dutch oven over medium-high heat. When the oil is hot, add the wonton squares a few at a time, without crowding them. As they turn golden, after 30 to 40 seconds, remove them with tongs and place them on a platter or baking sheet lined with paper towels. Repeat until all are cooked, reducing the heat if they are browning too quickly.

When ready to serve, place a few microgreens on each wonton square, top with a teaspoon of the diced ahi, sprinkle with the sesame seeds, and finish with a dollop of the sauce.

MAKES ABOUT 40 BITE-SIZE APPETIZERS, ENOUGH FOR 10 TO 15 SERVINGS

1 pound ahi (yellowtail) tuna steak, sashimi grade
½ cup mayonnaise
2 tablespoons (about 1½ limes) freshly squeezed lime juice
½ teaspoon sea salt
1 tablespoon prepared *harissa* paste
10 wonton wrappers, 3 by 3½ inches
Safflower or other oil for frying
½ cup microgreens or baby arugula or fresh basil leaves
¼ cup black sesame seeds

garlic-grilled shrimp

When the shrimp are grilled on the spot, guests tend to gather around the barbecue, reveling in the fragrance of the garlic, holding their plates out to be filled with the tasty crustaceans. Shrimp with the heads and tails intact are the most flavorful, and these are the ones I purchase. Besides the flavor, they look fresh and beautiful on the grill and on the plate. Since this is the main course, I prepare a lot of shrimp, and I serve plenty of bread to accompany it.

Wash and dry the shrimp, gathering them up in a clean cotton kitchen towel. In a large bowl, combine the olive oil, salt, pepper, garlic, and parsley. Stir to mix well, and add the shrimp, turning them to coat them well with the oil mixture.

Build a wood or charcoal fire in a grill, or preheat a gas grill. When the coals are hot or the grill reaches 400°F, put a layer of shrimp in a grilling basket and grill, turning with a spatula, until the shrimp are just pink and the meat is opaque, 3 to 4 minutes. Be careful not to overcook. Remove the shrimp to a serving platter garnished with lemon slices. Repeat until all the shrimp are cooked. Serve hot.

MAKES 12 TO 15 SERVINGS

10 pounds whole shrimp, heads and tails intact, about 25 per pound
⅓ cup extra-virgin olive oil
2 tablespoons coarse sea salt or kosher salt
2 tablespoons freshly ground black pepper
10 cloves garlic, minced
½ cup minced fresh flat-leaf parsley
4 lemons, thinly sliced

garlic-grilled shrimp

oven-roasted nectarines with crema and toasted pistachios

These make an elegant bite-size finish to the meal. Look for small nectarines, but if you can find only large ones, cut them into quarters. Peaches, plums, or figs can also be used. One of my neighbors grows organic pistachio nuts, and I like to use them as a topping, but you could use walnuts, almonds, or hazelnuts instead. The day before making the dessert, infuse the olive oil with the vanilla bean. The fresh crema is available at most Mexican groceries.

⅓ cup mild extra-virgin olive oil
1 vanilla bean
½ cup chopped pistachios
15 small nectarines, halved and pitted
8 ounces Mexican *crema* or sour cream

A day or two before the party, pour the olive oil into a jar with a lid. Slit the vanilla bean and scrape the seeds into the olive oil. Add the bean. Cover the jar and let it sit at room temperature.

Preheat the oven to 400°F.

Place a dry, nonstick frying pan over medium heat. When it is hot, add the chopped pistachios, and, while shaking the pan constantly, toast the nuts until they become fragrant, about 5 minutes. Set the nuts aside.

Remove the vanilla bean from the olive oil. Put the nectarine halves in a bowl, pour the oil over them, and mix gently to coat the fruit with the oil. Line a baking sheet with parchment paper and arrange the nectarines on it, cut side down.

Roast the nectarines until they are just caramelized, about 10 minutes. Remove the pan and let them cool to room temperature. Turn the nectarines cut side up and arrange them on a serving platter. In the center of each nectarine half, place a dab of the *crema* and sprinkle with some toasted pistachios.

MAKES 30 NECTARINE HALVES, ENOUGH FOR 10 TO 15 SERVINGS

fall

a vintner's feast

ROASTED RED PEPPER TOASTS WITH ITALIAN TUNA

PORK SHOULDER BRAISED IN ZINFANDEL

PURÉE OF CELERY ROOT AND POTATOES WITH CHANTERELLES

GARLIC-SAUTÉED CHARD

WALNUT-ALMOND TART

table setting for a vintner's feast

the party

Each autumn in Provence, my friends Pascal and Adele give a big grape harvest party, gathering all their friends and relatives together to help pick the grapes and stomp them. Theirs is a small vineyard, with only about seventy-five vines, but that doesn't diminish the extent of the food and fun. The meal starts at noon on a Saturday or Sunday, with aperitifs and appetizers, followed by the harvest.

Typically, Pascal, who is a wonderful cook, will serve several entrées that reflect the bounty of his world, such as bowls of braised wild boar, wild hare with just-collected mushrooms, platters of pan-seared sea bass, gratins of potato and onion, roasted vegetables, and salads from his garden, all well-seasoned with wild herbs, garlic, and olive oil. Myriad cheeses are laid out, and guests bring desserts, some homemade, but mostly from local patisseries. The previous year's vintage is drunk with the meal, and the vintage to come is toasted.

Although my husband, Jim, makes wine, we don't grow our own grapes, so a harvest party at home in California is symbolic, and we hold it after the grapes have been crushed and are fermenting. Fall is the time for hearty comfort foods that celebrate the new season, cooler now, and its different crops. Like Pascal, from whom I have learned so much over the years, I prepare an autumn meal based on the seasonal produce of my garden, a meal that is reflective of my world.

Decorating tips: I like to fill a gathering basket with bunches of grapes, their graceful leaves still attached, and place it on my sideboard. I add a few burnt-orange persimmons from my trees along with some walnut leaves, which, by late September and early October, are turning golden. Fall's fruit and foliage are so richly colored and textured, little else is needed.

Cooking tips: Braises are best made a day or two before serving, which leaves you extra time to enjoy your guests, since all you have to do just before the party is to gently reheat the braise and prepare the potatoes and chard. You can prepare the pie the morning of the party, as well as the toasts and roasted red peppers. Assemble them half an hour before your guests arrive. To simplify, you can purchase the dessert and skip the celery root and potato purée. To augment the meal and time spent at the table, include a final cheese course.

roasted red pepper toasts
with italian tuna

In my garden, fall is the best time of all for sweet peppers. They are juicy, thick, and meaty—perfect for roasting. If fresh sardines are available, I'll grill them to serve with the peppers, but tuna or anchovies packed in olive oil are always a safe bet.

Roast the peppers over an open flame or under the broiler until they are charred on all sides. Put them inside a plastic bag for 10 minutes, then peel off the skins. Cut the peppers in half and remove the seeds and ribs. Cut them into ½-inch-thick strips.

Drain the tuna and crumble it with a fork in a bowl. Add the lemon juice and capers. Mix gently, but do not mash them together.

Lay a strip or two of red pepper on each toast, and top with about a teaspoon of the tuna. Arrange the toasts on a platter.

To serve, sprinkle the toasts and some of the platter with the minced parsley, and squeeze the juice from the lemon wedges over the toasts.

MAKES 24 APPETIZERS, ENOUGH FOR 8 SERVINGS

3 large red bell peppers
4 ounces olive oil–packed Italian tuna in tins or jars
¼ cup (about 2 lemons) freshly squeezed lemon juice, plus ½ lemon cut into thin wedges
2 tablespoons capers, drained
1 baguette, cut into 24 slices about ¼ inch thick, toasted
¼ cup minced fresh flat-leaf parsley

pork shoulder braised in zinfandel

My husband makes both a zinfandel and a Rhône-style blend, so I make this dish with either wine; but at my house in Provence, I'd use one of the many local Rhône blends produced by nearby wineries. The key to this succulent dish is to let the pork cook slowly, slowly, in the wine and aromatics until it can be cut with a fork. I sometimes add fresh or dried mushrooms, or other vegetables such as carrots. I serve the pork with potatoes, pasta, or polenta.

Preheat the oven to 325°F.

Put 1½ tablespoons of the butter and olive oil in a Dutch oven or other heavy-bottomed, ovenproof pot with a lid, and place it over medium heat. When the butter foams, increase the heat to medium-high. Season the meat with some of the salt and pepper and brown it, a few pieces at a time, on all sides. Remove the browned meat to a bowl and continue until all the meat is browned, using about half the salt and pepper.

Pour off all but 1 tablespoon of the fat. Add the onion and garlic to the pot and sauté just until the onion has softened, about 1 minute. Pour in the wine, scraping up any browned bits clinging to the bottom of the pot. Add the carrots, celery, parsley, thyme, bay leaves, and the remaining salt and pepper.

Cover the pot and put it in the oven. Cook, stirring from time to time, until the pork is tender enough to cut with a fork, 2½ to 3½ hours.

When the pork is done, take it out of the oven and remove the carrots, celery, parsley, thyme, and bay leaves; discard. Remove the meat to a bowl. The sauce should be thickish and not watery. If it is too thin,

2½ tablespoons unsalted butter, divided

1½ tablespoons extra-virgin olive oil

3½ pounds pork shoulder (also sold as pork butt), cut into 2-inch pieces

1½ to 2 teaspoons coarse sea salt or kosher salt

1½ to 2 teaspoons freshly ground black pepper

¾ cup chopped onion

4 cloves garlic, chopped

½ bottle (about 2 cups) zinfandel, Rhône-style, or other red wine

2 medium-size carrots, cut in half

2 ribs celery, cut in half

4 sprigs fresh flat-leaf parsley, plus 1 tablespoon minced, for garnish

3 sprigs fresh thyme, plus 1 teaspoon minced thyme, for garnish

2 fresh bay leaves

1 tablespoon Dijon mustard

pork shoulder braised in zinfandel,
and purée of celery root and
potatoes with chanterelles

bring the sauce to a boil and let it reduce before adding the remaining butter and the mustard, whisking to make a smooth sauce. Return the meat to the sauce, bring it to a steaming heat, then transfer to a warm serving bowl. Garnish with a sprinkling of thyme and parsley and serve.

MAKES 8 SERVINGS

purée of celery root and potatoes with chanterelles

Adding celery root (also called celeriac) to mashed potatoes adds flavor as well as lightens them a bit. In the fall, chanterelle season, I always like to include some of these mushrooms in a meal, either with potatoes or other vegetables, as part of the entrée, or as a side dish. I'm using Yukon Gold potatoes for this recipe because we have some left from our spring harvest, but you could use any variety of waxy potato.

Peel the potatoes and cut them into 2-inch pieces. Trim the top and bottom of the celery root. If it has fresh leaves attached, remove them and save them for the garnish. Using a small, sharp knife, remove the thick skin of the celery root and discard it. Rinse the celery root and cut it into 2-inch pieces.

Put the potato and celery root pieces in a large saucepan and cover by 2 inches of water. Add 1 teaspoon of the salt and bring to a boil over high heat. Reduce the heat to medium-high and cook until the potatoes and the celery root are easily pierced with the tip of a knife.

Drain the vegetables and return them to the hot saucepan. Add about ½ cup of the milk and 1 tablespoon of the butter, or ½ tablespoon each of the butter and olive oil. Mash the vegetables with a potato masher until all the milk is absorbed. If you want a creamier purée, add more milk, a little at a time, until it is just short of the consistency you want to achieve (the mushrooms will add some liquid as well.). Add another ½ teaspoon of salt along with the pepper. Cover the pan and set it aside.

2 pounds Yukon Gold or other waxy potatoes

1 celery root, about 1 pound

2 teaspoons coarse sea salt or kosher salt, divided

½ to 1 cup hot milk

2 tablespoons unsalted butter, or 1 tablespoon olive oil plus 1 tablespoon unsalted butter, divided

½ teaspoon freshly ground black pepper

½ pound chanterelles, cleaned

Slice or quarter any large chanterelles, leaving the small ones whole. Melt the remaining butter, or the butter and olive oil, in a skillet over medium-high heat. When the butter foams, add the mushrooms and sprinkle them with about ¼ teaspoon of the remaining salt. Sauté until the mushrooms are tender and release their juices, 2 to 3 minutes.

Using a slotted spoon, transfer the mushrooms to the mashed potato mixture and stir them together. Taste for seasoning and adjust with the remaining salt as needed, adding a little more milk if desired. Cover the pan and keep the purée hot until you are ready to serve.

MAKES 8 SERVINGS

garlic-sautéed chard

I consider chard and other greens a necessity in my fall and winter garden, so I always have plenty on hand. They make an excellent accompaniment to the season's rich stews and braises.

Bend the chard if needed so it will fit into a large pot. Add about 5 inches of water to the pot and bring it to a boil over high heat. Add the rosemary sprigs. Reduce the heat and cover. Simmer until the stalks of the chard are tender, about 15 minutes. Remove the chard and rinse and drain it. Discard the rosemary sprigs. Coarsely chop the stalks and leaves of the chard and squeeze out any excess water.

Heat the olive oil in a saucepan over medium heat. When it is hot, add the garlic and the chard, and sauté until the garlic is golden and the chard shiny with the oil, about 5 minutes. Stir in the salt and pepper. Remove the pan from the heat and keep covered until you are ready to serve. The chard will stay hot for about 15 minutes, or you can gently reheat it.

MAKES 8 SERVINGS

4 bunches Swiss chard, trimmed
2 sprigs fresh rosemary
3 tablespoons extra-virgin olive oil
2 cloves garlic, minced
½ teaspoon coarse sea salt or kosher salt
½ teaspoon freshly ground black pepper

walnut-almond tart

Across the road from my house, and bordering our country roads, there are expansive walnut orchards. I watch them throughout the year, following their season from leaf to harvest, which occurs in September. By fall, I am using fresh, new-crop walnuts in everything from salads to desserts. This dessert is reminiscent of the nut tarts that appear in pastry-shop windows in Provence each autumn, and it is a perfect finish to a harvest meal.

Preheat the oven to 350°F.

Combine the corn syrup, eggs, sugar, butter, vanilla, walnuts, and almonds, and mix well with a spoon.

Line a 9-inch tart or pie pan with the piecrust. Pour the filling into the pan.

Bake until the crust is golden and the filling is firm, about 55 minutes to 1 hour.

Remove the tart from the oven and let it stand for 10 to 15 minutes before serving.

MAKES ONE 9-INCH TART, ENOUGH FOR 8 SERVINGS

½ cup light corn syrup
3 eggs
1 cup sugar
2 tablespoons unsalted butter, melted
1 teaspoon pure vanilla extract
1½ cups broken walnut pieces
¼ cup chopped almonds
1 unbaked piecrust for a 9-inch tart or pie

day of the dead

QUESADILLA TRIANGLES FILLED WITH SPICY CHEESE

CHICKEN IN GREEN MOLE SAUCE

CILANTRO RICE

DEAD MEN'S BONES COOKIES

MEXICAN CHOCOLATE SORBET WITH TOASTED ALMONDS

table decoration for day of the dead

the party

In Mexico and in Latino communities in the United States, Day of the Dead, or Día de los Muertos, is celebrated with much color and joy. Altars, or *ofrendas*, are set up at grave sites or at home to honor the dead. Favorite foods and drinks of the deceased are placed on the altars, along with photos, letters, and flowers. Decorating the altars are comical folk-art skeletons performing daily tasks; these figures are made of papier-mâché, clay, or wood, or are depicted in detailed paper cutouts.

It is a time to remember loved ones who are no longer with us, giving truth to the old saying that no one is truly dead until there is no one left to remember them. Families gather to reminisce, eat, and celebrate on November 1 and 2. The Mexican roots of the holiday are based in the ancient Aztec religion, which was overlaid with the Catholic All Hallows' Eve and All Saints' Day. While Halloween is meant to be scary, Día de los Muertos is a joyful holiday.

By mid-October in San Francisco's Mission District, a heavily Latino neighborhood where Ethel lives with her family, the bakeries are filled with special pastries and confections formed into fantastical shapes, from tombstones to bats, and store windows are set with skeleton dioramas, all brightly colored in reds, yellows, golds, blues, and pinks.

The Day of the Dead has taken on great personal meaning for me. Not long after my brother died unexpectedly, an old friend of his now living in Mexico wrote to tell me that she had made a Day of the Dead altar for him, which included some old letters and poems. I was deeply touched, and now, in a small way, I want to carry on the tradition. Since my brother loved good food, a gathering for the Day of the Dead seems a fitting way to honor his memory.

Decorating tips: You can go wild here, with everything from skeletons to tombstones, but go with the bright pinks, oranges, and yellows that you'd find in Mexico for the flowers and tableware, rather than Halloween orange and black. In Latino markets at this time of year, you can buy skulls made of colored sugar and sweet morning breads (*pan dulces*) shaped like plump, smiling little people (*cuerpos*) that represent the dead; these make good party favors and decorations.

Cooking tips: You could purchase a chocolate cake or chocolate ice cream instead of making the sorbet. If you are feeling really ambitious, serve miniature tacos, tamales, and salsa along with the quesadilla triangles.

quesadilla triangles filled with spicy cheese

Quesadillas, folded-over flour tortillas with a light filling, make a simple appetizer to set the mood of the gathering. Sometimes I add some crumbled cooked chorizo to the cheese, omitting the chipotle powder.

On a griddle or dry frying pan, warm a tortilla, turning it once or twice, to make it pliable. Remove and sprinkle half of it with some of the cheese, green onions, and chili powder. Fold over the other half and set aside. Repeat with the remaining tortillas.

In a frying pan over medium-high heat, heat just enough oil to film the bottom of the pan. When it is hot, fry the quesadillas one at a time, turning them once, until they are lightly browned and the cheese has melted, about 2 minutes. Keep warm until all the quesadillas have been cooked. Cut each of the quesadillas into 5 wedges, and serve hot.

MAKES 50 APPETIZERS, OR ENOUGH FOR 8 TO 10 SERVINGS

Ten 12-inch flour tortillas
3 cups (about ½ pound) grated Monterey Jack cheese
2 cups (about 3 bunches) minced green onions
3 to 4 teaspoons chipotle chili powder
Oil for frying

chicken in green mole sauce

Moles, savory sauces thickened with nuts and seeds, are a specialty of Mexican cooking, and there are many different regional varieties. For this dish, chicken is simmered in a fragrant broth and then covered with a rich green mole. Romaine lettuce and green Anaheim chiles give it color, and the seeds, nuts, and tortilla pieces thicken it. It is simple but authentic, and it makes a brilliant centerpiece for a casual gathering.

Prepare the chicken first, as you will need the broth that results from cooking the chicken to prepare the mole sauce. The chicken can be cooked up to a day in advance, but the sauce should be made no more than 2 or 3 hours before serving.

TO PREPARE THE CHICKEN

Place the chicken pieces in a stockpot and cover with about 12 cups of water. Add the onions, pepper, ginger, carrots, chile peppers, and salt. Bring to a boil over high heat, then reduce the heat to medium and simmer, uncovered, until the chicken is tender, about 1 hour and 15 minutes. If necessary, add a little more water to ensure being left with 8 cups of the broth. Remove the chicken from the broth, cover, and set aside. Strain the broth, reserving 3 cups for the mole sauce and 5 cups for the Cilantro Rice (page 119).

TO PREPARE THE MOLE SAUCE

Put the Anaheim and serrano chile peppers on a hot griddle or under a broiler and roast them, whole, until the skin is charred on all sides, 3 to 5 minutes. Place them inside a plastic bag and set them aside.

Put the tomatillos on the griddle or in a dry frying pan over medium heat and toast them until they just start to soften, about 2 minutes.

CHICKEN

1 chicken, about 4 pounds, cut into 8 serving pieces
1½ medium-size yellow onions, cut into quarters
2 teaspoons freshly ground black pepper
2-inch piece fresh gingerroot, peeled
2 carrots, halved
2 serrano chile peppers, halved and seeded
2 teaspoons coarse sea salt or kosher salt

MOLE SAUCE

4 green Anaheim chile peppers
2 serrano chile peppers
4 tomatillos, papery husks removed
3 cups reserved chicken broth, divided
2 tablespoons canola or sunflower oil
1 tablespoon hulled pumpkin seeds
2 teaspoons sesame seeds
8 blanched almonds

(CONTINUED)

Remove the chile peppers from the bag and peel them. Cut them in half and remove the seeds and ribs. In a blender or food processor, blend the chile peppers and tomatillos with 1 cup of the chicken broth. Set the mixture aside for 15 minutes to allow the flavors to develop.

Heat the oil in a frying pan over medium-high heat. When it is hot, add the pumpkin seeds, sesame seeds, and almonds, stirring until fragrant and just turning pale gold, 2 to 3 minutes. Place them in a blender or food processor, along with the chile mixture, the garlic, onion, bell pepper, peanut butter, allspice, and tomato.

Add ½ cup of the chicken broth and purée. Add the parsley, lettuce, and tortilla pieces and purée again. The mixture will now be bright green and somewhat thick. The consistency depends on how much moisture was in the vegetables. If the sauce is too thick, add a little bit more broth. If too thin, add more tortilla pieces, a little at a time. Ideally, you will use about 2 to 2½ cups of broth, and the sauce will have the consistency of thick cream.

In a saucepan over medium heat, heat the sauce until it turns a darker green, 10 to 15 minutes. Taste and season with salt.

TO ASSEMBLE AND SERVE

Preheat the oven to 350°F. Arrange the chicken pieces in a baking dish, cover with foil, and reheat until fully warmed, about 30 minutes. Transfer the chicken to a deep serving platter or bowl and pour the sauce over it. Serve immediately along with Cilantro Rice and warm tortillas.

MAKES 8 TO 10 SERVINGS

2 cloves garlic

½ medium-size yellow onion

1 medium-size green bell pepper, stemmed, seeded, and chopped

1 tablespoon unsalted peanut butter

2 whole allspice berries

1 tomato, chopped and seeded

1 cup chopped fresh parsley

1 large head romaine lettuce

1 small corn tortilla, torn into coarse pieces

½ to 1 teaspoon coarse sea salt or kosher salt

cilantro rice

One of the pleasures of a good mole sauce is soaking up every drop with rice and tortillas, and my green mole sauce is no exception. The bright green flecks in the rice reflect the sauce, making for a festive presentation. Use reserved broth from the Chicken in Green Mole Sauce (page 117) to cook the rice.

Melt the butter over medium-high heat in a stockpot. When it foams, add the onion and sauté until nearly translucent, 2 to 3 minutes. Add the rice and stir, cooking until the rice is glistening and becoming opaque, 2 to 3 minutes. Add the broth, water, salt, and pepper. Bring to a boil, then reduce the heat to very low and cover. Cook until the rice is tender and easily fluffed with a fork, about 20 to 25 minutes. Add the cilantro, mix gently, and serve.

MAKES 8 TO 10 SERVINGS

2 tablespoons unsalted butter
½ cup minced onion
5 cups long-grain white rice
5 cups reserved chicken broth
5 cups water
1 teaspoon coarse sea salt or kosher salt
1 teaspoon freshly ground black pepper
½ cup minced fresh cilantro leaves

dead men's bones cookies

Butter cutout cookies are one of my standby desserts. I have an extensive cookie-cutter collection, including some that I've bent into various shapes to suit my needs, such as a star that became an almond tree. If I don't have the proper cutters, I make my own cardboard templates.

In the spirit of the Day of the Dead, I've made templates that resembled curved rib bones, femurs, and even a few finger bones. Once the cookies are baked and cooled, I decorate them with white icing and white or silver sprinkles, and then serve them piled on a platter.

⅔ cup unsalted butter, at room temperature
½ cup sugar
1 egg
1¾ cups all-purpose flour
½ teaspoon baking powder
¼ teaspoon fine sea salt
Royal Icing (recipe follows)
White or silver sprinkles for decorating

Preheat the oven to 400°F.

Using a food processor, pulse the butter and sugar together until fluffy, about 2 minutes. Add the egg and pulse several times to blend.

Whisk together the flour, baking powder, and salt in a bowl. Add the flour mixture to the butter mixture in 3 portions, pulsing briefly after each addition, until the flour is absorbed and a soft ball of dough forms, about 2 minutes total.

On a lightly floured board, roll out the dough to a thickness of about ⅛ inch. Using cookie cutters or templates, cut the dough into the desired shapes and arrange them 1½ inches apart on ungreased baking sheets.

Gather up the scraps and form them lightly into a ball. Roll out the dough as before, and continue cutting cookies until you have used up all of the dough.

Bake until the cookies are just lightly browned on the bottom and pale golden on top, 6 to 8 minutes.

Remove from the oven and let the cookies cool on the baking sheets for 5 minutes. With a spatula, transfer the cookies to a work surface. Thinly spread the cookies with the Royal Icing, and while it is still moist, scatter the sprinkles on top. Let the icing dry completely before serving or storing the cookies.

MAKES ABOUT 36 FINGER-SIZED COOKIES

royal icing

This is a simple and versatile icing for cookies. You can spread it with a knife or pipe it, and you can tint it with liquid or gel food coloring. It is best used right after making. If you are concerned about serving raw egg whites, you can use the packaged pasteurized egg whites instead.

2 egg whites
4 cups confectioners' sugar, more
  as needed

Beat the egg whites and the sugar together in a large bowl, using an electric mixer. Beat until the mixture is stiff enough to spread, about 10 minutes. If the icing is too stiff, add 1 teaspoon of water and beat some more. If the icing is too thin, add additional confectioners' sugar, up to ¼ cup, and beat until blended.

MAKES ABOUT 1½ TO 2 CUPS

*mexican chocolate sorbet
with toasted almonds*

mexican chocolate sorbet
with toasted almonds

Mexican chocolate is premixed with sugar and, usually, cinnamon, and is ready to melt into milk or water for champurado, *the hot frothy drink beloved in Mexico. Here I've used Mexican chocolate as the base of a sorbet, adding almonds, although you could use other nuts instead. You may need to freeze this in two batches, depending on the size of your ice cream maker. The sorbet can be made several days ahead.*

In a saucepan over medium-high heat, combine the water, sugar, and cocoa powder, whisking well to blend.

Melt the chocolate in the top of a double boiler set over medium-high heat, stirring to prevent it from burning. Once the chocolate has melted, stir it into the cocoa mixture, along with the salt, vanilla, and almonds.

Let the mixture cool to room temperature, then chill it, covered, for 4 hours. Freeze in an ice cream maker according to the manufacturer's directions.

MAKES ABOUT 2 QUARTS, ENOUGH FOR 8 TO 10 SERVINGS

4 cups water
½ cup sugar
1 cup good-quality unsweetened cocoa powder, preferably Dutch process
12 ounces Mexican chocolate (with sugar and cinnamon), finely chopped
Pinch of salt
½ teaspoon pure vanilla extract
1 cup toasted, coarsely chopped almonds

poker night

ROASTED NUTS WITH ROSEMARY

TRI-TIP WITH BLACK PEPPER RUB

SPICY OVEN FRIES

OLD-FASHIONED MACARONI SALAD

DEEP-DISH APPLE PIE

poker night

the party

I've always enjoyed a good poker game, even if the stakes are only dried beans! I'm quite competitive and not a bad player. My best game ever was one winter night in Florence, Italy, playing with a group of Fulbright scholars. I was winning heavily, and I harbored a fantasy that one of the men, who was losing, would offer to bet the necklace of antique uncut garnets that he had shown off earlier in the evening.

He didn't. Instead, he just stopped playing, but I've never forgotten how exotic and beautiful that necklace was, and how enthralled I was by its Italian provenance. Also beautiful that night were the foods we ate—the sumptuous pasta, the meats and cheeses, and the simple red wine we drank with our meal. In that spirit, here is a simple meal to serve on Poker Night, or any other evening that your friends gather for games and fun, from Scrabble to bridge.

Decorating tips: Keep it simple, since the focus is really on the game. Use a colorful tablecloth, wrap each set of cutlery in a cloth napkin, and set them on the table or buffet along with the dishes and a big basket of rolls or different breads.

Cooking tips: Some markets sell delicious precooked tri-tip roasts, which, if you are rushed, you might buy instead of cooking your own. However, although it's easier to buy it ready-made, I'd stick with a homemade macaroni salad, which is a real treat, as is the homemade apple pie. For a large gathering, you could add a baked ham and potato salad, as well as an extra pie.

roasted nuts with rosemary

These rosemary-spiced nuts are perfect little treats for snacking on during the game, and they go well with wine or cocktails.

Preheat the oven to 350°F.

Scatter the almonds on a baking sheet in a single layer, then drizzle them with the olive oil and sprinkle with the sea salt and rosemary. Turn them with your hands or a wooden spoon to mix them well. Tuck the sprigs of rosemary among them and roast the nuts until fragrant and light golden brown inside, turning several times, about 30 minutes (about 10 minutes for cashews).

To see if the nuts are golden, after about 20 minutes, cut a nut in half to check. Remove from the oven and let them cool completely. To store, place the almonds, along with the rosemary sprigs, in an airtight container for up to 3 weeks, or in the freezer for up to 1 month.

MAKES 4 CUPS

4 cups (about 20 ounces) almonds or cashews
4 tablespoons extra-virgin olive oil
3 teaspoons coarse sea salt or kosher salt
1 tablespoon finely minced fresh rosemary, plus 5 or 6 sprigs

tri-tip with black pepper rub,
and spicy oven fries

tri-tip with black pepper rub

Tri-tip, sometimes called "triangle roast" because of its shape, is a relatively inexpensive cut, but it is deliciously tender and takes well to all kinds of rubs and marinades. This pepper rub is simple and yields a tasty crust. I think it is just right for a poker party—not too fussy, but hearty.

Trim the meat of excess fat, leaving a thin layer. Mix the salt, pepper, and garlic together and rub it all over the roast. Let the meat stand at room temperature for 2 hours, or cover and refrigerate overnight.

Preheat the oven to 350°F.

Pat the roast dry if necessary. If it has been refrigerated, bring it to room temperature before cooking. Place the roast fat side up on a rack in a small roasting pan. Roast it until a crust forms and the internal temperature, when tested with an instant-read thermometer inserted into the middle of the roast, reads 120°F for rare or 125°F to 130°F for medium rare, 30 to 40 minutes.

Transfer the roast to a carving board, cover it loosely with foil, and let it rest for 15 minutes. Carve the meat across the grain in ¼-inch-thick slices. Arrange the slices on a platter and pour any collected pan juices over them. Serve immediately.

MAKES 6 TO 8 SERVINGS

1 tri-tip or small sirloin roast, about 1¾ to 2 pounds
1½ teaspoons coarse sea salt or kosher salt
2½ teaspoons freshly ground black pepper
2 teaspoons minced garlic

spicy oven fries

Spicy fries like these are served, hot from the oven, at Spanish tapas bars as a snack to be washed down with beer or wine, but I also like them as a side dish with roasted meats.

Preheat the oven to 350°F.

Cut the potatoes lengthwise into wedges about ½ inch wide. Put them in a bowl and toss well with the olive oil. Mix the salt, pepper, and chili powder together and sprinkle the mixture over the potatoes. Turn, distributing the spices.

Place the potato wedges in a single layer on a baking sheet. Bake until the bottoms of the potatoes start to turn brown and the tops form a skin, about 20 minutes. Turn the potato wedges over and bake until the potatoes are golden brown, crisp outside and soft inside, about 20 more minutes. Serve hot or warm.

MAKES 8 SERVINGS

8 russet potatoes, skins left on
4 tablespoons extra-virgin olive oil
1 tablespoon coarse sea salt or kosher salt
1 tablespoon freshly ground black pepper
1 tablespoon chili powder

old-fashioned macaroni salad

My mother used to make macaroni salad for my father, who loved it, as we all did, and I've tried to recapture the flavor of her recipe here. I doubt she used capers, but I think they create the "bite" that I remember, along with the sharp sweetness of the pickles. She served it with Southern-style fried chicken, something I've never managed to cook to my satisfaction, but the salad works just as well as a hearty side dish for the Tri-Tip with Black Pepper Rub (page 129). You can prepare the salad a day ahead.

Heat a large pot of water over medium-high heat. Add the macaroni and cook until tender. For this salad, softer is better than al dente. Drain it well; extra water that gets trapped in the elbows will dilute the dressing.

Put the drained macaroni in a large bowl and add the mayonnaise, mustard, pickles, pickle juice, olives, onions, capers, parsley, salt, and pepper. Turn well with a wooden spoon until thoroughly mixed. Taste and add more salt if desired.

Put the salad into a serving bowl, garnish with the eggs, and sprinkle with the paprika. Cover and refrigerate until ready to serve.

MAKES 8 SERVINGS

2 cups small elbow macaroni

6 tablespoons mayonnaise

2 teaspoons Dijon mustard

5 tablespoons minced sweet pickles, plus 1 teaspoon pickle juice

4 tablespoons minced pimiento-stuffed green olives

2 tablespoons minced red onions

2 tablespoon capers, drained

2 tablespoons minced flat-leaf parsley

½ teaspoon coarse sea salt or kosher salt

½ teaspoon freshly ground black pepper

2 hard-cooked eggs, sliced

1 teaspoon mild paprika

deep-dish apple pie

If you serve this old-fashioned fruit-laden pie warm, perhaps with a scoop of vanilla ice cream or wedges of sharp cheddar cheese, you'll have a grand conclusion for your dinner. I use the Granny Smith apples from my trees, but you can certainly use other varieties of your choice.

TO PREPARE THE PIECRUST

Put the flour, salt, and butter in the bowl of a food processor and pulse just until the mixture has a coarse, grainy texture. Add the vinegar and sugar and pulse briefly to blend. Add the ice water a little at a time while pulsing, using only as much water as needed until a rough ball begins to form. Remove the dough and divide it into 2 balls, one slightly larger than the other. Wrap them in plastic wrap and refrigerate for at least 4 hours.

When you are ready to prepare the pie, remove the larger ball of dough from the refrigerator, unwrap it, and let it stand at room temperature for 15 to 20 minutes in order to soften.

Preheat the oven to 350°F.

On a lightly floured work surface, roll out the dough into a disk about 13 inches in diameter and ¼ inch thick. Loosely drape the pastry over the rolling pin and transfer it to a 9-inch deep-dish pie pan. Press the dough gently into the pan, leaving at least a ½-inch overhang, and place it in the refrigerator while you prepare the apple filling. Remove the smaller ball of dough from the refrigerator and let it soften while you work.

PIECRUST

2 cups all-purpose flour

1 teaspoon coarse sea salt or kosher salt

¾ cup (1½ sticks) very cold unsalted butter, cut into pieces

2 teaspoons distilled white vinegar or cider vinegar

2 tablespoons sugar

½ cup ice water, approximately

APPLE FILLING

4 pounds Granny Smith or other apples, peeled, cored, and cut into ¼-inch-thick slices

2 teaspoons (about 1 lemon) finely grated fresh lemon zest

1½ teaspoons freshly squeezed lemon juice

¼ cup firmly packed brown sugar

⅓ cup granulated sugar

⅓ cup all-purpose flour

½ teaspoon freshly ground cloves

¼ teaspoon freshly grated nutmeg

4 tablespoons (½ stick) unsalted butter, cut into small bits

TO PREPARE THE FILLING

Combine the apples, lemon zest, and lemon juice in a large bowl. Add the sugars, flour, cloves, and nutmeg and mix well. Spoon the filling into the chilled piecrust, heaping it higher in the center. Scatter the bits of butter over the top.

Roll out the smaller ball of dough into a disk of about 11 inches in diameter and ¼ inch thick. Drape the pastry loosely over the rolling pin and place it on top of the apples. Tuck the edge of the upper crust under the lower, pinching them together to seal well. Make 3 or 4 slashes, about 1 inch long, in the upper crust to allow the steam to escape.

Place the pie on a baking sheet to catch any drips, and bake until the crust is golden brown, the apples are tender, and the filling is bubbling, 45 to 50 minutes. Remove the pie from the oven and let it cool on a rack for 45 minutes before serving. Serve warm or at room temperature.

MAKES ONE 9-INCH PIE, ENOUGH FOR 6 TO 8 SERVINGS

an elegant thanksgiving with turkey

LOBSTER SALAD TOASTS WITH TARRAGON

CREAM OF MUSSEL SOUP WITH CANDIED ORANGE PEEL

ROAST TURKEY WITH CORNBREAD, WALNUT, AND DRIED FRUIT STUFFING
AND GIBLET GRAVY

GARDEN WALDORF SALAD WITH BLUE CHEESE

BRUSSELS SPROUT CHIFFONADE WITH CARAMELIZED SHALLOTS

OLD-FASHIONED MINCEMEAT PIE

the party

I find Thanksgiving is most memorable when our family is joined by those my children call "strays"—people whose families live far away or who have no immediate family. Consequently, over the years our Thanksgiving table has included a number of our children's adult friends, visitors from out of town, and our own friends who decided not to travel over the holidays, making for an interesting mix and providing many helping hands.

Now the family table includes grandchildren, who follow the Thanksgiving tradition of plucking ripe olives to put on their fingers from the ceramic lazy Susan made by their great-grandfather, and sampling cranberry sauce from their great-grandmother's crystal bowl.

I like a traditional meal with a big turkey—and I cook the stuffing inside the bird. We always have a lot of side dishes and plenty of leftovers afterward. Champagne starts off the celebration, or sometimes I'll serve old-fashioned and Manhattan cocktails, in memory of my mother and father-in-law. I always serve some classic appetizers, such as the ever-popular clam dip and potato chips, celery stuffed with pimiento cream cheese, or molded shrimp and celery spread.

Next comes a special soup or salad course and at least one exotic appetizer. With the meal, I usually serve a white wine along with one of my husband, Jim's, reds. We conclude with coffee and pie. There must be a pumpkin pie, made with homemade pumpkin purée, and—my new favorite—a pie of made-from-scratch old-fashioned mincemeat.

Decorating tips: In October, I'll collect autumn leaves in beautiful colors and press them between several thicknesses of newspaper, weighted with books, for a week or so, then scatter them on the dinner table. On the sideboard, I place an arrangement with persimmons, pomegranates, and winter squash or gourds.

Cooking tips: Thanksgiving is an occasion where the food dominates, so use your prettiest serving dishes and utensils to showcase it. You can delegate some of the dishes, such as the onions and sweet potatoes or the pie, to family members or friends, while you take care of the rest. For this elegant, traditional meat menu, the creative emphasis is on the mussel soup and the turkey and stuffing. For large groups, plan on several pies, including perhaps pecan and apple.

lobster salad toasts with tarragon

After you have made the fumet, or stock, for the Cream of Mussel Soup (page 138), use the remaining lobster meat for this elegant appetizer. Brioche is a buttery, tender bread often served with French delicacies such as lobster and foie gras. If you can't find it, you can substitute challah. The lobster salad topping also makes a delicious filling for gougères (see page 53). The lobster can be prepared in the morning, and the toasts can be assembled and served whenever you are ready.

Tear (but do not shred) the lobster meat into chunks small enough to fit on the toasts. Mix together the crème fraîche, shallots, salt, white pepper, tarragon, olive oil, and cayenne, then gently fold in the lobster. Cover and refrigerate until ready to serve.

Preheat the oven to 400°F.

Arrange the brioche triangles on a baking sheet. If you are using baguette slices, brush them lightly with extra-virgin olive oil. Toast them in the oven until pale gold, about 5 minutes. Turn and toast the other side, about 5 minutes. Do not overbake. To serve, spread a little of the lobster salad on each toast.

MAKES 16 TO 20 APPETIZERS, ENOUGH FOR 8 SERVINGS

Meat from 1 large or 2 small lobsters, 2½ to 3 cups
3 tablespoons crème fraîche
2 tablespoons minced shallots
½ teaspoon fine sea salt
½ teaspoon freshly ground white pepper
1 tablespoon minced fresh tarragon
1 teaspoon extra-virgin olive oil
¼ teaspoon cayenne
5 to 6 slices brioche, trimmed, cut into triangles, or 16 to 20 thin slices of baguette

cream of mussel soup with candied orange peel

This is probably the most delicious soup I have ever tasted, but of all the soups I've made, it is also the most complex. It was first served to me by the remarkable young chef at a restaurant in Forcalquier, a historic market town in Haute-Provence. I was entranced by the soup and the restaurant, and I would take my cooking students there, urging them to try the soup, although everything the chef prepared was exceptional. One day I found the courage to ask him how he made it, and he sweetly wrote out the recipe for me.

I served the soup at our next Thanksgiving dinner. Ethel, Mary Ann, and others helped me to get it just right. And it was Mary Ann who devised the lobster salad (see page 137) made with the leftover lobster meat.

We did the entire preparation on Thanksgiving Day, but I suggest taking your time over two days.

This soup pairs beautifully with a glass of Beaumes de Venise, the remarkable muscat wine of Provence's Rhône Valley. The French chef and I determined, after much sampling of various wines, that this unusual choice, which echoes the orange in the soup, was a perfect match.

TO PREPARE THE CANDIED ORANGE PEEL

Strip off the outer peel only from about half the orange in long, thin strips.

Bring the water and the sugar to a boil in a saucepan. Add the orange strips, reduce the heat to low, and cook until they have absorbed some of the syrup and become translucent, about 45 minutes.

Remove the strips and set them on a rack to dry. This can be done a day or two ahead. Once the orange strips are dry, roll them in sugar. Store in an airtight container in a dry location for up to 1 week.

CANDIED ORANGE PEEL

1 medium-size orange, preferably organic or unsprayed

1 cup water

1 cup sugar, plus more for rolling peel

FUMET (STOCK)

1½ quarts (6 cups) water

1 medium-size yellow onion, quartered

1 carrot, quartered

5 whole black peppercorns

2 bay leaves

4 sprigs fresh thyme

5 sprigs fresh parsley

1 large or 2 small live lobsters

¼ cup extra-virgin olive oil

SOUP

2½ cups dry white wine

2½ pounds live black mussels, scrubbed, rinsed, debearded

1½ quarts (6 cups) heavy cream

1½ teaspoons dried saffron threads

cream of mussel soup with
candied orange peel

TO PREPARE THE FUMET

Combine the water, onion, carrot, peppercorns, bay leaves, thyme, and parsley in a large stockpot over medium-high heat and bring to a boil. Add the live lobster and cook for 20 minutes.

Remove the lobster from the pot, leaving the fumet in the pot. Crack the lobster shells and remove the meat, but do not discard the shells. Reserve the lobster meat, covered in the refrigerator, for the Lobster Salad Toasts with Tarragon (page 137) or another use.

Heat the olive oil in a frying pan and add the lobster shells, sautéing them well over medium heat for about 15 minutes. Add the shells to the stockpot and simmer, uncovered, for about 1 hour. Remove and discard the shells. The fumet can be prepared up to this point a day ahead.

TO PREPARE THE SOUP

Add the white wine to the stockpot and bring the fumet to a boil over high heat. Discard any mussels whose shells remain open even when you tap them gently against another, and discard any that feel especially heavy, as they may be sandy. Lower the heat to medium, add the live mussels to the stockpot, cover, and cook just until they have all opened, 5 to 10 minutes. Remove the mussels, reserving the fumet. Discard any mussels that remain closed at this point.

Remove the mussels from their shells and put them in a bowl. Moisten them with some of the fumet and cover the bowl with plastic wrap. Set aside.

Simmer the fumet over medium heat and let it reduce by about half, about 20 minutes. Stir in the cream and saffron and continue to cook, reducing again by about half, about 20 to 30 minutes longer. The soup should now be thick and creamy. Strain it through a *chinois* or extra-fine mesh strainer into a clean pot.

Mince the candied orange peel into small pieces.

Add the mussels and the orange peel to the soup and heat to just below a boil. The soup should be served quite hot. Ladle it into shallow, rimmed soup bowls, about ½ to ⅔ cup per serving. Serve immediately.

MAKES 8 TO 10 SERVINGS

roast turkey with cornbread, walnut, and dried fruit stuffing and giblet gravy

Stuffing is my favorite part of Thanksgiving dinner. Over the years, I've made many versions, using chestnuts, oysters, and even chorizo. This is the one I like best, and that my son, Oliver, still expects me to serve each year. Some of the elements vary, but cornbread, nuts, and dried fruits are the basics. Lately we've been drying our Thompson Seedless grapes to make raisins, and sometimes I dry my own figs as well, and I will use these in the stuffing. Gravy is a key component in the meal, and we all insist on enough of the dark, giblet-rich gravy to spoon over hot turkey sandwiches the next day. The turkey we get is a large, free-range one that we purchase from a local turkey farmer, ordering it ahead and picking it up a day or two before cooking it.

TO PREPARE THE STUFFING

Put the baguette cubes into a large bowl and pour 1 cup of the chicken broth over the bread to soften it. Turn the bread several times and let stand.

Melt 2 tablespoons of the butter over medium-high heat in a pan or pot large enough to hold all of the stuffing. When the butter foams, add the onion and celery, and reduce the heat to medium. Sauté until the onion is translucent and the celery soft, 6 to 7 minutes.

Add the bread mixture, the sage, thyme, parsley, and hot water, and stir well to moisten the bread. Add the cornbread and continue to mix. Add the remaining butter, the figs, apricots, walnuts, salt, and pepper, and mix well. The stuffing should be soft and somewhat sticky. If it is too dry and crumbly, add a little more broth until you have the desired consistency.

STUFFING

4 cups dried 1-inch bread cubes, cut or torn from leftover sliced baguette, *pain au levain,* or other coarse-crumbed bread

1 to 3 cups chicken broth

3 tablespoons unsalted butter, divided

1 cup chopped onion

1 cup (about 4 ribs) chopped celery

2 tablespoons minced fresh sage

1 tablespoon minced fresh thyme

¼ cup minced fresh parsley

2 cups hot water

2 to 3 cups day-old 1-inch cubes cornbread

10 to 12 dried figs, hard stem tips removed

10 to 12 dried apricot halves

½ cup chopped walnuts

1 to 1½ teaspoons coarse sea salt or kosher salt

½ teaspoon freshly ground black pepper

Remove the pan from the heat, cover, and set the stuffing mixture aside while you prepare the turkey.

TO PREPARE THE TURKEY

Preheat the oven to 325°F.

Remove the giblets and neck from the cavity of the turkey and reserve them. Discard the liver or reserve it for some other use. Pat the turkey dry with paper towels. Season the cavity with the salt and pepper.

Fill the chest cavity with the stuffing, but do not pack it tightly.

With kitchen string, tie the legs together. Turn the turkey over and fill the neck cavity with stuffing, tucking the skin flap over the stuffing and fastening it with a skewer.

Rub the butter over the breast, thighs, legs, and wings. Place the turkey, breast side up, on a rack in a roasting pan just large enough to hold it. If, while roasting, the wings brown too quickly, tuck some aluminum foil over them to protect them. While the turkey is roasting, start making the giblet gravy.

Roast the turkey until an instant-read thermometer inserted into the thickest part of the thigh, but not touching the bone, registers 170°F to 175°F, and the stuffing temperature is 160°F. Plan on 12 to 15 minutes per pound for a stuffed turkey. A 19-pound turkey will be done in about 3 to 3½ hours. In any case, use and trust your thermometer.

When the turkey is ready, transfer it to a cutting board. Snip the strings and remove all of the stuffing from the chest and the neck cavities. Put the stuffing into serving bowls, cover them with aluminum foil, and keep warm. Tent the turkey loosely with aluminum foil and let it rest 20 to 30 minutes before carving.

TURKEY

1 turkey, 16 to 19 pounds, fresh or thawed, with giblets
1½ teaspoons coarse kosher or sea salt
1½ teaspoons freshly ground black pepper
½ tablespoon unsalted butter, at room temperature

GRAVY

Turkey neck and giblets
1 medium-size yellow onion, coarsely chopped
1 small carrot, peeled and coarsely chopped
1 rib celery, coarsely chopped (about ¼ cup)
1 bay leaf
2 sprigs fresh parsley
4 whole black peppercorns
1½ cups dry white wine, such as sauvignon blanc
⅓ cup unsalted butter
⅓ cup all-purpose flour
Salt

TO PREPARE THE GRAVY

Put the reserved turkey neck and giblets in a large saucepan. Add the onion, carrot, celery, bay leaf, parsley, and peppercorns. Cover them by 4 inches with cold water and bring to a boil over high heat. Skim off any foam that arises while cooking. Reduce the heat to low, partially cover the pan, and simmer until the giblets are tender, about 2 hours, adding more water if needed.

Remove the pan from the heat and strain the broth through a sieve set over a bowl or measuring pitcher. Reserve the giblets and neck, and discard the vegetables, herbs, and peppercorns. Finely chop the giblets and, if you wish, remove the meat from the neck bone; set aside. You should have about 3 cups of broth. Return the strained broth to the saucepan, set it over high heat, and boil until the broth reduces to 1½ cups, about 15 minutes.

After the turkey is done roasting, while it is resting, pour all of the pan juices from the roasting pan into a bowl or a fat separator. Skim off and discard the fat, and reserve the pan juices.

Set the roasting pan over medium heat, using 2 burners if necessary. Pour the pan juices and the wine into the roasting pan. Increase the heat to high and stir, scraping up any of the browned bits that are clinging to the bottom of the pan. Let the liquid reduce to about 3 cups. Strain it through a mesh sieve set over a bowl or pan.

Melt the butter in a saucepan set over medium heat, and stir in the flour, making a smooth paste. Slowly pour in the reduced broth and then the reserved pan juices, whisking constantly to make a smooth gravy. Add the reserved giblets and meat, if desired, and stir. Season the gravy to taste with salt and keep it warm while you carve the turkey.

MAKES 16 TO 18 SERVINGS

garden waldorf salad with blue cheese

This salad, which originated at New York's Waldorf-Astoria Hotel at the end of the nineteenth century, was a favorite of my mother's and was frequently on the Thanksgiving table during my childhood. Today I make it with the late-harvest Granny Smith apples from my trees, local walnuts, and celery from my garden, laced together with a mayonnaise-based dressing lightly flavored with blue cheese.

In a small bowl, mix together the mayonnaise, milk, sugar, vinegar, salt, and blue cheese, mashing the cheese with a fork. The dressing should be the consistency of heavy cream. Add more mayonnaise and milk, as needed, to achieve the right consistency.

Put the apples in a mixing bowl and squeeze the lemon juice over them. Add the celery and half of the walnuts. Spoon the dressing over all and mix gently, turning well to coat. Transfer the salad to a serving bowl and garnish with the remaining walnuts. Cover with plastic wrap and refrigerate up to 2 hours before serving.

MAKES 10 SERVINGS

½ cup mayonnaise, plus more as needed

3 tablespoons whole milk, plus more as needed

2 teaspoons sugar

2 teaspoons white wine vinegar

¼ teaspoon fine sea salt

2 ounces crumbled blue cheese

6 Granny Smith apples, cored and diced

Juice of 1 lemon (2 to 3 tablespoons)

6 ribs (about 1½ cups) celery, finely chopped

½ cup toasted walnut pieces, divided

brussels sprout chiffonade
with caramelized shallots

I consider brussels sprouts an essential part of Thanksgiving and Christmas dinner, and I prepare them in various ways each year. They are a specialty of the cool, coastal areas near Half Moon Bay, about 90 miles southwest of my home. When possible, I buy the whole stalk on which they grow, looking like tiny cabbages on a club. Cooking them in the same pan in which you caramelize the shallots adds extra flavor to this dish.

Preheat the oven to 350°F.

In an ovenproof frying pan or sauté pan with a lid, heat 1 tablespoon of the butter with the olive oil over medium-high heat. When the butter foams, add the shallots and half the salt, and sauté until the shallots just begin to turn golden, about 3 minutes. Cover the pan, reduce the heat to low, and cook, stirring from time to time, until the shallots are a rich, golden brown.

Add the remaining butter, increase the heat to medium-high, and add the brussels sprouts and the remaining salt, stirring until the sprouts become limp, 2 or 3 minutes. Increase the heat to high, add the wine, and scrape up any browned bits clinging to the bottom of the pan.

Cover the pan and place it in the oven. Cook until the brussels sprouts are tender, about 15 minutes.

Remove the pan from the oven. Season the sprouts with the pepper and drizzle them with the oil, turning several times. Serve hot.

MAKES 10 SERVINGS

2 tablespoons unsalted butter, divided

1 tablespoon extra-virgin olive oil

2½ large shallots, thinly sliced (about ½ cup)

1½ teaspoons coarse sea salt or kosher salt, divided

2½ to 3 pounds fresh brussels sprouts, cut lengthwise into chiffonade

⅔ cup dry white wine, such as sauvignon blanc

1 teaspoon freshly ground black pepper

1 tablespoon walnut oil, butter, or extra-virgin olive oil

old-fashioned mincemeat pie

I've made mincemeat frequently over the years, but this recipe, adapted from an old English recipe in the booklet Favourite Country Preserves *by Carol Wilson, makes an unforgettable mincemeat. My business partner and friend and I made it together, starting two months before Thanksgiving because the flavors need one to three months to develop. We used some of Jim's grappa rather than the traditional brandy. It was by far the favorite of the several pies I served at Thanksgiving, and I intend to make it every year from now on.*

I believe that candying your own lemon and orange peel is key to the amazing flavor and fragrance. I also recommend that you grind your own spices—it makes a dramatic difference. You can order the beef suet from your butcher. For best results, prepare the mincemeat in September, allowing it two months to mellow, but it should be prepared at least one month in advance. I also like to offer Perfect Pumpkin Pie (page 161) alongside this one as an alternative.

TO PREPARE THE MINCEMEAT

Combine the apples, suet, raisins, currants, sultanas, candied orange and lemon peels, almonds, lemon zest and juice, sugar, allspice, nutmeg, cinnamon, and ginger in a large bowl. Stir them well together until thoroughly mixed. Cover the bowl and leave it overnight, at room temperature, for the flavors to blend.

The next day, preheat the oven to 225°F. Stir the mixture well, pour it into a baking pan, and cover the pan with aluminum foil. Bake the mincemeat for 3 hours. Remove the pan from the oven and let the mincemeat cool, stirring occasionally until all the ingredients are coated in the melted suet. When the mincemeat is completely cold, stir in the brandy. Pack into sterilized jars, cover, and keep in the refrigerator until ready to use. (The mincemeat will keep for up to 6 months.)

MINCEMEAT FILLING

1 pound Granny Smith or other tart apples, unpeeled, cored and chopped

8 ounces shredded beef suet

12 ounces raisins

8 ounces Zante currants

8 ounces sultana raisins

4 ounces Candied Orange Peel, chopped (recipe follows)

4 ounces Candied Lemon Peel, chopped (recipe follows)

1⅓ cups slivered or chopped almonds

Grated zest and juice of 1 lemon

12 ounces dark brown sugar

2½ teaspoons freshly ground allspice

½ teaspoon freshly grated nutmeg

½ teaspoon freshly ground cinnamon

½ teaspoon freshly ground dried ginger

7 tablespoons brandy

TO PREPARE THE PIECRUST

Combine the flour, salt, and butter in a food processor and pulse until the mixture just reaches a coarse, grainy texture. Add the vinegar and sugar and pulse briefly to blend. Add the ice water a little at a time while pulsing, using only as much water as needed until a rough ball begins to form. Divide the dough into 2 balls, one slightly larger than the other, wrap them in plastic, and refrigerate for at least 4 hours.

When you are ready to prepare the pie, unwrap the balls of dough and let them stand at room temperature for 15 to 20 minutes to soften.

Preheat the oven to 400°F.

On a lightly floured board, roll out the larger of the balls into a disk about 13 inches in diameter and ¼ inch thick. Line a 9-inch pie pan with the pastry, letting it hang over the edge, and press it gently into the pan. Fill the pie with about 1 quart (4 cups) of the mincemeat filling, heaping it up slightly in the center.

Roll out the smaller ball of dough into a disk about ¼ inch thick, and cut it into ½-inch-wide strips. Brush the rim of the pastry lining the pie pan lightly with water, and lay some of the pastry strips across the pie filling about 1 inch apart in one direction. Place more strips going the other direction, again about 1 inch apart, making a latticework. Brush the pastry strips with the egg yolk.

Bake until the piecrust is a pale bisque color, about 30 minutes, then reduce the heat to 350°F and continue baking until the filling is bubbling and the crust is golden brown, 30 to 40 minutes longer.

PIECRUST

2 cups all-purpose flour
1 teaspoon salt
¾ cup (1½ sticks) very cold unsalted butter, cut in pieces
2 teaspoons distilled white vinegar or cider vinegar
2 tablespoons sugar
½ cup ice water, approximately
Water for brushing piecrust
1 egg yolk, beaten, for brushing piecrust
Whipped cream, for serving

Remove the pie from the oven and set it on a rack to cool. Let the pie cool completely before serving with whipped cream. The pie can be made several days ahead, wrapped well, and refrigerated. Reheat the pie in a 250°F to 300°F oven for about 20 minutes before serving.

MAKES ONE 9-INCH PIE, ENOUGH FOR 10 SERVINGS

candied orange or lemon peel

Seville oranges were probably used in England for the original mincemeat recipes. If you can't obtain these prized Spanish oranges, use Valencia or navel oranges. As for lemons, the common Lisbon or Eureka lemon varieties are most desirable for candying, as the Meyer lemon peel is very thin and delicate.

You can prepare the candied peels well ahead of time, as they store well in airtight containers. You will need to make one full batch of candied orange peel and one of candied lemon peel for the mincemeat pie. Prepare the batches separately to ensure the peels keep their distinct flavors.

3 oranges or lemons
3 quarts (12 cups) plus 2 cups water, divided
1½ cups sugar, divided

Cut a thin slice from the top and bottom of each fruit. Cut vertically through the outer skin to the fruit inside, spacing the cuts about 1 inch apart. Peel the citrus, reserving the fruit for another use.

Cut each section of peel lengthwise into wide 1-inch strips.

Combine the citrus strips with the 3 quarts water in a saucepan over high heat. Bring to a boil, then reduce the heat to medium. Cook, uncovered, until only 1 inch or so of water remains in the pan, about 1 hour. Using a slotted spoon, remove the strips from the pan and set them aside in a bowl. Discard the liquid.

Combine the 2 cups water with 1 cup of the sugar in a nonreactive saucepan. Bring it to a boil over high heat, stirring until the sugar dissolves completely. Remove the pan from the heat and stir the still-warm strips into the syrup. Let them stand for 1 to 2 hours at room temperature.

Return the pan to low heat and cook the strips until they have absorbed all of the syrup, about 30 minutes. They will become translucent and amber in color. During the last stages of cooking, keep a close eye on them to prevent scorching or burning.

When the peel is done cooking, remove it from the pan and arrange it on a piece of waxed paper or kitchen parchment. Sprinkle the remaining sugar on top, and roll the peel in the sugar to cover completely. Let the candied peel stand overnight, then put it in an airtight container and store it in a dry place for up to 2 weeks.

MAKES ABOUT 4 OUNCES

a vegetarian thanksgiving feast

CRUDITÉS WITH GARLIC HUMMUS

GIGANDES WITH WILD ARUGULA AND MEYER LEMON ZEST

TWICE-BAKED BUTTERNUT SQUASH WITH WALNUT AND DRIED FRUIT STUFFING

BALSAMIC-ROASTED ONIONS

BRAISED LACINATO KALE

WATERCRESS AND FRISÉE SALAD WITH SHAVED PARMESAN AND QUAIL EGGS

PERFECT PUMPKIN PIE

the party

My holiday table often includes many of the vegetarian options provided here, and combined, these festive dishes create a full and flavorful menu to satisfy any vegetarian who sets to it with a knife, fork, and spoon. A trick with vegetarian meals, however, is to have one centerpiece dish that stands out above the others, and I think that the Twice-Baked Butternut Squash with Walnut and Dried Fruit Stuffing (page 156) here accomplishes that. The meal is completed with a traditional and delicious pumpkin pie.

Decorating tips: To reflect the dishes prepared for this vegetarian feast, it is especially attractive to compose a display of different shapes, sizes, and colors of winter squashes, such as the Cinderella red pumpkin; the buff, deeply lobed *Musquée de Provence* pumpkin; and the pale grey-green Australian pumpkin. Intersperse the squash with autumn leaves and even branches.

Cooking tips: Cook the beans and onions the day before, along with the pumpkin purée. The hummus can be made a day ahead as well. On Thanksgiving morning, prepare the pie. This will free up your oven for the twice-baked squash to be finished right as you serve the meal. Just before serving, heat the *gigandes*, taste for seasonings, and add the arugula and lemon zest. By timing your preparations as suggested, this becomes an uncomplicated menu that even a novice cook can handle alone.

crudités with garlic hummus

This is an easy dip to put together, and it goes well with the assortment of fall vegetables that surround the platter. You can use as many different kinds of vegetables as you'd like to enhance the color and presentation.

Drain and rinse the garbanzo beans. Put them in a blender or food processor with the garlic, 2 tablespoons of the olive oil, the paprika, cumin, and lemon juice, then purée. If it is too thick, drizzle in some of the remaining olive oil a little at a time to produce a creamy consistency. Taste and add salt as desired.

Peel the carrots and cut them in half crosswise, then quarter them lengthwise. Divide the broccoli and cauliflower into florets. Trim the ends of the black radishes, then cut them into thin slices.

Spread the hummus on a platter surrounded by the crudités. Drizzle the hummus with a little olive oil and sprinkle lightly with paprika. Serve the hummus at room temperature.

MAKES 10 SERVINGS

Two 13-ounce cans garbanzo
  beans
4 cloves garlic, coarsely chopped
2 to 4 tablespoons extra-virgin
  olive oil
1 teaspoon mild paprika, plus
  more for garnish
½ teaspoon cumin seeds
1 teaspoon freshly squeezed
  lemon juice
Salt
4 carrots
3 broccoli crowns
2 heads cauliflower
2 black or red radishes

gigandes with wild arugula and meyer lemon zest

Gigandes, *also called* gigantes, *or giant white beans, are the biggest, fattest, meatiest beans ever, with a deep, rich flavor. They are grown near California's Half Moon Bay. I buy them at San Francisco's Ferry Plaza Farmers Market, but you can also find them at Greek and Mediterranean specialty markets and online, or you can substitute Spagna, flageolet, or cannellini beans, which are much smaller but delicious and maintain their integrity when cooked.*

Wild arugula is a strain of the more common garden arugula. Its sage-green leaves have deeply serrated edges and intense flavor. It grows like a weed in my garden, so I keep it thinned to just one or two plants that supply me with all I need. If it is unavailable, substitute young, bright-green garden arugula.

Pick over and rinse the beans. In a large pot over high heat, combine the water, beans, half the salt, the bay leaves, and rosemary sprigs, and bring to a boil. Reduce the heat to low and cover the pot. Simmer, stirring from time to time, until the beans are tender to the bite and the liquid has reduced to about 8 cups, about 2 hours. Remove the bay leaves and rosemary springs. Add the pepper and taste, adding more salt if desired.

Ladle the beans with a little broth into warm bowls. Garnish with the arugula and lemon zest and serve immediately.

MAKES 10 SERVINGS

3 cups (about 1 pound) *gigande,* Spagna, flageolet, or cannellini beans

15 cups water

3 teaspoons coarse sea salt or kosher salt

2 bay leaves

2 sprigs fresh rosemary

4 teaspoons freshly ground black pepper

45 (about ½ cup) small wild arugula leaves, coarse stems removed, chopped into thin slivers

2½ tablespoons (about 3 lemons) coarsely grated Meyer lemon zest

twice-baked butternut squash with walnut and dried fruit stuffing

This makes a festive main-dish presentation for your vegetarian guests, and it is full of the flavors of autumn. I especially like the taste and texture of the dried pears and peaches, but you could use other fruits instead, such as dried apples. Baking the squash twice allows you to use some of the pulp in the stuffing, which makes it fluffy and light, while the rest becomes soft and succulent in the shell. Look for the smallest butternut squash you can find so you can offer half a squash per person, but if only large ones are available, cut them into quarters to serve.

Preheat the oven to 350°F.

Place the squashes on a baking sheet and bake until they offer little resistance when pierced with a toothpick, about 1 to 1½ hours, depending on size.

Remove and let the squashes cool to room temperature, about 1 hour. (They can be baked the day before and left at room temperature, covered.)

Preheat the oven again to 350°F.

Carefully cut the squash in half lengthwise. With a metal spoon, scrape out the strings and seeds and discard. Scrape out the pulp, which will still offer a little resistance, to within ½ inch of the shell. Chop or mash the pulp and set aside.

Melt the butter in a frying pan over medium-high heat. When it foams, add the onions and celery and sauté until translucent, about 2 minutes. Add the sage, parsley, bread, peaches, prunes, pears, walnuts, squash pulp, broth, salt, and pepper.

5 small butternut squashes, each about 1 pound
5 tablespoons unsalted butter
1¼ cups minced onion
6 ribs (about 1½ cups) celery, minced
4 tablespoons minced fresh sage
¼ cup minced fresh flat-leaf parsley
8 to 10 large slices *pain au levain* or other coarse-crumbed bread, crusts removed, torn or cut into small pieces
8 dried peach halves, finely chopped
12 prunes, finely chopped
8 dried pears, finely chopped
1¼ cups chopped walnuts
1½ to 2 cups vegetable broth
1½ teaspoons coarse sea salt or kosher salt
1½ teaspoons freshly ground black pepper

Reduce the heat to low and simmer to make a moist mixture, about 5 minutes. If the stuffing seems too dry, add a little more broth. Taste and add more salt and pepper if desired.

Fill the squash cavities with the stuffing, mounding it generously. Cover each squash separately with aluminum foil, pressing it to fit snugly. Put the squash on a baking sheet and bake again until the meat of the squash shell is tender when pierced with a fork, about 1 hour. Remove the foil and serve hot.

MAKES 10 SERVINGS

balsamic-roasted onions

These onions are rich and sweet and make a nicely balanced accompaniment to the stuffed butternut squash. They can be made a day ahead, then gently warmed before serving. Add a tablespoon or two of water to augment the sauce, because the onions will have absorbed some.

Peel the onions, keeping the stem end intact. Slice the onions in half lengthwise if small, in quarters if medium in size.

In a large frying pan or sauté pan set over medium-high heat, melt 4 tablespoons of the butter until it foams. Gently place the onions, cut side down, in the pan. They should fit snugly in a single layer. Reduce the heat to medium, add the salt and pepper, and gently simmer for 6 to 7 minutes until they soften, but do not let them brown.

Add the water and the balsamic vinegar and continue to simmer another 3 to 4 minutes. Gently turn the onions. With the remaining butter, grease the parchment and place it buttered side down on top of the onions. Cover the pan and reduce the heat to low. Simmer, turning several times, until the onions are tender and very soft, about 40 minutes. Remove the cover and the parchment. Taste and adjust for salt and pepper, if necessary. Serve the onions immediately, or transfer them to a bowl to cool. Cover and refrigerate for up to 24 hours. Reheat before serving.

MAKES 10 SERVINGS

8 small to medium-size yellow onions

4 tablespoons plus 1 teaspoon unsalted butter, divided

½ teaspoon coarse sea salt or kosher salt

¼ teaspoon freshly ground black pepper

2 tablespoons water

¼ cup balsamic vinegar

1 piece kitchen parchment, cut to fit the interior of your frying or sauté pan

braised lacinato kale

Italian lacinato kale, also called dinosaur or "dino" kale in the United States, is the secret ingredient in true minestrone soup. Its beautiful long, dark-green, narrow leaves are heavily savoyed, or crinkled, quilted in puffs and curling slightly inward. With a milder flavor than most kale varieties, it is a standby in my fall and winter garden, where it thrives. It can be found at farmers markets and some produce and specialty markets.

Remove the long, tough ribs from the kale by folding and holding the edges together, with the rib exposed, then pulling the rib from the bottom to the top of the leaves. Discard the ribs. Coarsely chop the leaves.

In a saucepan set over medium-high heat, bring the broth to a boil. Add half of the salt and pepper and the chopped kale. Reduce the heat to low, cover, and simmer until the leaves are tender, about 25 minutes. Drain, reserving the cooking liquid.

Put the kale in a serving bowl, sprinkle with the remaining salt and pepper, drizzle with the olive oil, and turn gently. Serve warm.

MAKES 10 SERVINGS

30 leaves (about 5 bunches) lacinato kale

5 cups chicken broth

2 teaspoons coarse sea salt or kosher salt

½ teaspoon freshly ground black pepper

2 tablespoons extra-virgin olive oil

watercress and frisée salad with shaved parmesan and quail eggs

Salads are, for me, an important part of every meal, and Thanksgiving is no exception. This salad is more formal than the Garden Waldorf Salad with Blue Cheese (page 145) on the Elegant Thanksgiving with Turkey menu, and it is meant to be served as a separate course following the soup. Quail eggs can usually be found at Asian markets, but you can substitute chicken eggs, cut into quarters, if you can't find them.

Put the quail eggs in a saucepan and cover with cold water. Bring the water to a boil, then remove the pan from the heat.

Let the eggs stand for 5 minutes, then remove them and let them cool in a bowl. Crack the eggs and gently peel them. Slice the eggs in half lengthwise and set them aside.

If using chicken eggs, follow the same procedure, but let them stand in the hot water for 20 minutes.

In a large salad bowl, combine the olive oil, balsamic vinegar, red wine vinegar, mustard, salt, and pepper. Mix well with a fork. Just before serving, add the watercress and frisée and toss well with the dressing to coat.

Divide the salad among 10 salad plates. Using a vegetable peeler, shave curls of the Parmesan cheese, and scatter 3 or 4 curls on top of each salad. Garnish each plate with 3 quail egg halves or 2 chicken egg quarters. Serve immediately.

MAKES 10 SERVINGS

18 quail eggs, or 5 chicken eggs

4 tablespoons extra-virgin olive oil

3 teaspoons balsamic vinegar

2 teaspoons red wine vinegar

1 teaspoon Dijon mustard

½ teaspoon coarse sea salt or kosher salt

¼ teaspoon freshly ground black pepper

2 bunches watercress, leaves and sprigs only, about 3 cups

4 heads frisée, pale inner yellow leaves only, torn into bite-size pieces, about 5 cups

3 ounces Parmesan cheese, in 1 piece

perfect pumpkin pie

This pie has a pumpkin purist's filling, made with homemade pumpkin purée and freshly ground spices. Baking pumpkins, such as Sugar Pie, yield the finest-grained, most flavorful purée. Jack-o'-lantern pumpkins have been bred primarily for carving and tend to be fibrous and flavorless.

Grinding the spices in a clean coffee grinder or spice mill gives the pie a wonderful, fresh flavor. (Before grinding spices in your coffee grinder, clean it of any lingering coffee oils. Put a tablespoon of uncooked rice into the grinder and whirl for a few seconds until it becomes a powder. Tap out the rice powder and wipe the grinder clean with a damp paper towel.) Do take this extra step, and your own senses, along with those of your guests, will be rewarded.

TO PREPARE THE PIECRUST

Combine the flour, salt, and butter in a food processor, and pulse just until the mixture has a coarse, grainy texture. Add the vinegar and sugar and pulse briefly to blend. Add the ice water a little at a time while pulsing, using only as much water as needed until a rough ball begins to form.

Divide the dough evenly into 2 balls and wrap them well in plastic wrap. Refrigerate one of the balls for at least 4 hours, and freeze the other for up to 1 month, well wrapped, for another pie.

Remove the chilled dough from the refrigerator, unwrap it, and let it stand at room temperature for 15 to 20 minutes to soften.

On a lightly floured work surface, roll out the dough into a disk about 13 inches in diameter and ¼ inch thick. Loosely drape the disk over the rolling pin and transfer the dough to a 9-inch deep-dish pie pan. Press the dough gently into the pan, leaving at least a ½-inch overhang. Chill the piecrust in the refrigerator until you are ready to fill and bake the pie.

PIECRUST

2 cups all-purpose flour
1 teaspoon salt
¾ cup (1½ sticks) very cold
    unsalted butter, cut into pieces
2 teaspoons distilled white
    vinegar or cider vinegar
2 tablespoons sugar
½ cup ice water, approximately

PUMPKIN FILLING

1 Sugar Pie pumpkin, about 2 or
    3 pounds
¾ cup sugar
½ teaspoon salt
1 teaspoon freshly ground
    cinnamon
½ teaspoon freshly ground dried
    ginger
½ teaspoon freshly ground cloves
2 eggs
1 cup evaporated milk
½ cup water

TO PREPARE THE PIE FILLING

Preheat the oven to 350°F.

Put the pumpkin on a baking sheet and bake until a sharp knife easily pierces through to the seed cavity, about 1 to 1½ hours. Remove the pumpkin from the oven and let it cool.

When it is cool enough to handle, peel the skin away with a knife. Cut the pumpkin in half, scoop out the seeds and fibers with a large spoon, and discard them (or save the seeds for roasting). Finally, mash the flesh to a creamy purée by hand with a potato masher or process it in a food processor.

The purée is now ready to use. Any leftover purée can be stored in an airtight container in the refrigerator for up to 4 days.

Increase the oven temperature to 450°F.

Cook the pumpkin purée in a large saucepan over medium heat for about 10 minutes, stirring until it becomes dry and begins to caramelize slightly. Stirring constantly to prevent sticking and burning, add the sugar, salt, cinnamon, ginger, and cloves to the purée. Remove the pan from the heat.

In a medium-size bowl, beat together the eggs, milk, and water, then beat this mixture into the pumpkin mixture.

Pour the filling into the pastry-lined pie pan. Crimp the edges of the pastry to make a decorative border. Bake the pie for 15 minutes. Reduce the oven temperature to 300°F and bake for about 45 minutes. Test the pie for doneness by gently shaking it to see how much of the center is still liquid. When only the center inch of the pie still jiggles, remove the pie from the oven—it will finish cooking outside of the oven. Let the pie cool on a wire rack for at least 20 minutes before serving.

MAKES ONE 9-INCH PIE, ENOUGH FOR 10 SERVINGS

winter

a book club buffet

CHICKEN SALAD SANDWICHES WITH CRANBERRIES AND ALMONDS

CITRUS SALAD WITH SPICY CANDIED WALNUTS

BUTTERNUT SQUASH SOUP WITH GREEN HERBS

CHOCOLATE BROWNIES

chicken salad sandwiches with cranberries and almonds

the party

People often think of winter as a dreary time of year, not suitable for entertaining, but I think this kind of casual menu—sandwiches, soup, salad, and a simple dessert—is perfect to serve on a dark winter day or evening, when a group of friends gets together in front of a roaring fire to knit, work on journals, or to discuss a favorite book. Since the menu is buffet style, people can eat and continue their work and conversation, the food being a tasty and satisfying background to the task at hand.

Decorating tips: I like to place a bowl of oranges and lemons on the buffet table, and a branch or two of flowering quince from my garden in a slender vase for an unfussy display.

Cooking tips: If you're short on time, ask one of the guests to bake the brownies or buy them at a favorite bakery. A guest could also bring focaccia or artisan bread for the sandwiches to save you a trip. And if you're sitting by the fireplace, warm and snug, you could forgo the soup and double the salad.

chicken salad sandwiches with cranberries and almonds

This is a chicken salad I started making when my children were small, substituting yogurt for a portion of the mayonnaise. The salad went with us on picnics and served as a filling for sandwiches or gougères (see page 53); I've even made bite-size versions in the hundreds for parties. Here I suggest chicken breasts, but the salad is also excellent when made with a whole roasted chicken, either purchased or home-cooked.

Preheat the oven to 350°F.

Pat the chicken breasts dry with a paper towel. Rub them with half of the salt and pepper. Place them in a pan and roast until the meat is opaque and the juices run clear when pierced with a fork, about 35 to 45 minutes.

Remove the pan from the oven and let the chicken cool. When it is cool enough to handle, remove and discard the skin. Remove the meat from the bones and cut it into ½-inch cubes.

Put the celery, green onions, and shallots into a large bowl, and add the chicken. Add the yogurt, mayonnaise, crème fraîche, almonds, cranberries, and the remaining salt and pepper, and turn to mix well. Taste and add more salt and pepper if desired. At this point, the salad can be covered and refrigerated for up to 24 hours.

To assemble the sandwiches, cut the focaccia into 8 equal-size rectangles, then cut each in half horizontally to make the top and

3 whole bone-in, skin-on chicken breasts (about 1½ pounds total)

1 teaspoon coarse sea salt or kosher salt, divided

1 teaspoon freshly ground black pepper, divided

2 ribs (about ½ cup) celery, finely chopped

2 green onions, including lower half of green tops, finely chopped

1 tablespoon minced shallots

¼ cup plain nonfat or low-fat yogurt

¼ cup mayonnaise

1 heaping tablespoon crème fraîche

¼ cup slivered almonds

2 tablespoons dried cranberries, coarsely chopped

1 sheet focaccia, about 9 inches by 14 inches

1 cup mixed garden lettuce

bottom part for each sandwich. Spread both sides of the bread with additional mayonnaise, if desired. Generously spread the chicken salad on the bottom half of each sandwich and cover with the top half. Slip a bit of lettuce into each sandwich. Serve immediately, or cover and serve within the hour.

MAKES 8 SANDWICHES

citrus salad with spicy candied walnuts

Winter is citrus season, and since oranges, tangerines, grapefruit, and other citrus go so well with winter's bitter greens, such as frisée and escarole, the combination is an obvious choice for me—especially because I have a number of citrus trees, as well as greens, growing in my garden.

Mix the olive oil, vinegar, and salt in a salad bowl. Add the shallots, then the orange and grapefruit segments.

Remove the pale inner leaves of the frisée and escarole and tear them into bite-size pieces. You should have about 4 tightly packed cups. If not, use some of the larger, greener leaves as well. Add the greens to the salad bowl. You can let this stand up to half an hour. When you are ready to serve, add half the walnuts to the salad and toss well. Garnish with the remaining walnuts and serve.

MAKES 8 SERVINGS

4 tablespoons extra-virgin olive oil

2 tablespoons white wine vinegar or Champagne vinegar

½ teaspoon coarse sea salt or kosher salt

2 tablespoons minced shallots

4 navel oranges, peeled, segmented, each segment cut in half

1 grapefruit, peeled, segmented, each segment cut in half

1 head frisée

1 head escarole

½ to ¾ cup Spicy Candied Walnuts (recipe follows)

citrus salad with spicy candied walnuts

spicy candied walnuts

These make a good pantry item to have on hand for salads and snacking. They will keep up to 2 weeks at room temperature, or up to 3 months in the freezer. Be sure to remove the nuts from the freezer an hour or so before serving.

In a small bowl, stir together the cayenne, sugar, salt, and ginger. Place the egg whites in another bowl and using a whisk or electric mixer, beat until frothy but not stiff.

Preheat the oven to 225°F.

Using a small brush or your fingertips, lightly brush each walnut half with a small amount of the egg white, then sprinkle it with the spice mixture. As each walnut is coated, place it on a kitchen parchment–lined baking sheet.

When all the walnuts are coated, place the baking sheet in the oven and bake until the nuts are toasted and crunchy and the coating is crispy, about 20 minutes.

Remove the pan from the oven and let the nuts cool completely. Pack the spiced nuts in an airtight container.

MAKES 3 CUPS

1 tablespoon cayenne
2 tablespoons sugar
1 teaspoon fine sea salt
¾ teaspoon ground ginger
6 egg whites
3 cups (about 12 ounces) walnut halves

butternut squash soup with green herbs

Everyone seems to like butternut squash soup, especially on a cold winter night. This is a very easy version that can be made in advance—simply reheat the soup gently and add the crème fraîche and herb garnish just before serving.

Using a sharp knife, cut the squash in half lengthwise, and scoop out and discard the seeds and stringy threads. Peel the squash and cut it into 1- to 1½-inch cubes. (Alternatively, cube the squash first, then cut away the skin.) Repeat with the other squash. You should have 3½ to 4 cups of squash.

Melt the butter in a large saucepan or soup pot set over medium-high heat. When it foams, add the shallots, reduce the heat to medium, and sauté until the shallots are translucent but not browned, about 2 minutes.

Add the chicken broth and thyme, increase the heat to medium-high, and bring to a boil. Add the squash, reduce the heat to low, and simmer until the squash is tender and easily pierced with a fork, about 20 minutes. Remove the pot from the heat.

Using an immersion blender, purée the soup until smooth. Or purée the soup in batches using a blender or food processor. Taste and add salt if desired.

Return the soup to the heat and warm through gently, if necessary. To serve, ladle into bowls and top each serving with a dollop of crème fraîche and a sprinkle of chives.

MAKES 8 SERVINGS

1 or 2 butternut squash (about 5 pounds total)
2 tablespoons unsalted butter
¼ cup minced shallots
6 cups chicken broth
1 teaspoon fresh thyme leaves
Salt
¼ cup crème fraîche
2 tablespoons snipped fresh chives

butternut squash soup with green herbs

table setting for a book club buffet

chocolate brownies

Everyone loves brownies, and if you use good-quality semisweet chocolate with the recommended 62 percent cacao or higher, these are especially good, with plenty of chocolate flavor. The brownies can be made the day before your party, covered snugly with plastic wrap or foil, and kept in a cool, dry place.

Preheat the oven to 350°F.

In a large mixing bowl, using an electric mixer or a wooden spoon, beat the butter until it is fluffy, then add the sugar. Beat to incorporate well. Add the eggs and vanilla and beat again until well blended.

Add about a third of the flour and the salt, and beat again. Add the remaining flour in two batches, beating well after each.

In the top of a double boiler set over boiling water, heat the chocolate, stirring until it has melted, about 2 minutes. Add it to the batter and beat until well blended and creamy.

With the remaining butter, grease a 9-inch square baking pan. Pour in the batter, spreading it evenly in the pan.

Bake until the brownies are puffed and a toothpick inserted into the center comes out clean, about 20 to 25 minutes. Do not overbake.

Place the pan on a cake rack and let cool. When the brownies are cool, cut them into squares.

MAKES 16 BROWNIES, ENOUGH FOR 8 SERVINGS

1 stick plus ½ teaspoon unsalted
   butter, at room temperature
1 cup sugar
2 eggs, beaten
1 teaspoon pure vanilla extract
¾ cup all-purpose flour
Dash salt
4 ounces semisweet baking
   chocolate, at least 62 percent
   cacao, broken or cut into
   small pieces

a cozy sunday supper

MARINATED MUSHROOMS

CHEESE FONDUE

MÂCHE AND BELGIAN ENDIVE SALAD

BLOOD ORANGE COMPOTE WITH STAR ANISE

the party

Winter is my favorite time of year for inviting a few good friends or family members to an early Sunday supper. It's dark by 5 p.m., just right for candlelight, and since I have a fireplace in my kitchen, I can build a nice fire in the late afternoon. The fire keeps me company while I prepare the last stages of the meal, and it is a cozy welcome for my guests.

A meal of cheese fondue is so convivial and lends itself to simplicity, requiring little more than the addition of a salad and an easy dessert, but I always like to have at least one appetizer to offer guests, along with my usual olives and nuts.

Although I often serve an appetizer of toasts with a spread, that would be too much bread for this menu, bread being an integral part of the fondue. Instead, marinated mushrooms are a good choice—not too heavy, but full of flavor, and a contrast in texture as well. In Provence, the local people harvest the wild mushrooms called *sanguins*. They cut the large ones in quarters (leaving the smaller ones whole), pickle them, and serve them along with an aperitif. Here I use our regular domestic button mushrooms. To end the meal, I've chosen a colorful blood orange compote that I like to serve with any simple homemade or purchased cookie.

Decorating tips: The fondue pot itself, sitting in the middle of the table, is the focus and primary decoration for this simple supper. I'd set out a bowl of oranges or tangerines with their glossy leaves still attached, and I'd light lots of candles to emphasize the warmth of being inside on a dark winter night. If my narcissus bulbs are in bloom, I'd gather some for a bouquet on the sideboard, but not on the table, because they are so fragrant they would over-whelm the food.

Cooking tips: I like to keep various preserved delicacies and condi-ments on hand for appetizers that I can serve on short notice, such as olives, anchovies, and assorted charcuterie. I would substitute a platter of these for the marinated mushrooms, if I didn't have time to prepare them or if I couldn't find the quality mushrooms I wanted.

marinated mushrooms

When choosing button mushrooms for this dish, look for small, bite-size, tightly closed mushrooms, with no dark gills showing, indicating that they are firm and fresh. These will hold up well to the marinade.

Trim off only any bruised ends of the mushroom stem, leaving the rest intact. Bring a saucepan of water to a boil and add 1 teaspoon of the salt. When the water is boiling, add the mushrooms and blanch for 45 seconds to 1 minute. Remove and drain the mushrooms well.

Combine the olive oil, 3 tablespoons of the vinegar, garlic, red pepper flakes, thyme, and bay leaves. Add the still-warm mushrooms and mix well to coat. Cool the mushrooms to room temperature, then refrigerate them for at least 6 hours and up to 12 hours before serving.

When ready to serve, bring the mushrooms to room temperature and taste the marinade. If it seems watery, as the mushrooms will have released some of their juices, add the remaining vinegar and salt and mix. Serve the mushrooms at room temperature, with toothpicks.

MAKES 8 SERVINGS

32 small, firm, tightly closed button mushrooms
2 teaspoons coarse sea salt or kosher salt, divided
⅓ cup extra-virgin olive oil
3 to 4 tablespoons red wine vinegar
2 cloves minced garlic
1 teaspoon crushed red pepper flakes
1 teaspoon minced fresh thyme leaves
2 bay leaves

cheese fondue

My good friend Georgette and her cousins, who live in the French Alps, taught me how to make this traditional fondue recipe, and I have used it ever since. "Buy the best cheese," Georgette told me, "or you'll be disappointed." And, as always, I follow her culinary advice. In line with the classic style I was taught, I serve only bread for dipping into the melted cheese. Be careful not to overcook the cheese, or it may begin to separate.

Crush the garlic cloves, thoroughly rub the interior of the fondue pot with them, and discard them when spent. Pour the wine into the fondue pot and set it over medium-high heat until bubbles appear along the inside of the pot.

Stir in the cheeses and heat, stirring occasionally, until they have almost completely melted, about 10 minutes. Add the nutmeg, reduce the heat to medium-low, and stir in the kirsch, salt, pepper, and butter, continuing to stir until the cheese has just melted, no longer.

To serve, light the alcohol, Sterno, or electric burner that accompanies the fondue pot and place it on the table. Put the fondue pot on top of it, and bring the bread cubes to the table. Everyone helps himself or herself to bread, spearing a cube with a fondue fork, then dipping and swirling it in the cheese.

MAKES 8 SERVINGS

5 cloves garlic

1 bottle dry white wine, such as Apremont, from Savoie, or a sauvignon blanc

1½ pounds Gruyère cheese, shredded or cut into thin slivers

½ pound Emmentaler cheese, shredded or cut into thin slivers

¼ teaspoon freshly grated nutmeg

¼ cup kirsch

½ teaspoon coarse sea salt or kosher salt

¼ teaspoon freshly ground black pepper

1 tablespoon unsalted butter

2 baguettes, cut into 1-inch cubes

cheese fondue

mâche and belgian endive salad

Jim and I first tasted this salad many years ago at a small restaurant on the Loire River in France. It was December, and the bright flavors of the crisp salad seemed to go perfectly with the weather. When I can't find mâche, I substitute watercress or arugula, but mâche (which is also known as lamb's lettuce or corn salad) is a much milder-tasting salad green.

In a salad bowl, combine the olive oil, lemon juice, and salt and mix with a fork. Taste, and adjust with lemon and salt as desired. The dressing should be light but not bland.

Using a paring knife, cut a ½-inch-deep cone from the base of each of the Belgian endive heads and discard the cores. Cut each head lengthwise into half-inch slivers.

Place the endive and the mâche in a plastic bag and refrigerate until you are ready to serve the salad. At that time, add them to the dressing and toss well to coat.

MAKES 8 SERVINGS

3 tablespoons extra-virgin olive oil
2 teaspoons freshly squeezed lemon juice
½ teaspoon coarse sea salt
4 or 5 heads Belgian endive
2 cups mâche sprigs, separated and cut if large

blood orange compote with star anise

Oranges were a luxury in the French Alps during my friend Georgette's child-hood, and they would not have appeared at a fondue dinner. I grew up in Southern California, where orange groves were everywhere, and oranges have always been part of my life. Now I have my own blood orange and navel orange trees here in Northern California. Since winter is the peak of citrus season, this compote seems an especially appropriate dessert.

8 blood oranges, or use navel
   oranges if necessary
1 cup water
1 cup sugar
3 whole dried star anise
¼ cup crème de cassis (optional)

With a zester or sharp knife, remove and reserve all the zest of 6 of the oranges, reserving the zest from half an orange to use for the garnish.

Peel the white pith from the zested oranges, then remove the peel and any pith from the remaining oranges. Remove the seeds and cut the oranges into generous ¼-inch-thick slices and arrange them in layers in a shallow serving bowl.

Put the water and sugar in a heavy-bottomed saucepan set over medium heat. Cook, stirring often, until the sugar dissolves, about 5 minutes. Add the larger quantity of zest and the star anise, reduce the heat to low, and simmer, uncovered, until a thick syrup has formed and the flavors have blended, about 1 hour.

Remove the pan from the heat and discard the zest. Stir in the crème de cassis. Pour the hot syrup over the orange slices. Cover and let stand at room temperature for at least 1 hour before serving, or up to 12 hours. If serving later, cover and refrigerate. To serve, cut the remaining zest into julienne and sprinkle it over the oranges.

MAKES 8 SERVINGS

christmas eve with carpaccio and cracked crab

BEEF CARPACCIO CURLS

CRACKED DUNGENESS CRAB WITH SPICY DIPPING SAUCE

SALAD OF BITTER GREENS WITH APPLE CIDER BALSAMIC VINAIGRETTE

HAZELNUT BÛCHE DE NOËL

table decoration for christmas eve
with carpaccio and cracked crab

the party

Christmas Eve, with all its excitement and expectation, is my favorite of the winter holiday season. I'm happiest when friends and family gather to share it, but one year I got more excitement than I expected. Ethel's new in-laws-to-be were coming from Paris to meet her family for the first time, and we had ordered oysters, Dungeness crab, Champagne, and plenty of fresh baguettes for the Christmas Eve feast. We had invited some local French friends and their children to join us as well—the perfect gathering.

However, on December 22, we had a fire at our house and the electricity had to be shut off, so I needed an emergency plan. I called my friend, and we decided to hold the party at her house, but I would be bringing the food.

My son, Oliver, and stepson Tom drove to San Francisco to pick up the freshly harvested seafood from a fishmonger there. I made a huge bowl of dipping sauce for the crab and picked lemons from our trees for the oysters. Jim ordered a cake from an Austrian baker to replace the *bûche de noël* I had planned but could no longer make. On Christmas Eve, our now-extended family bundled up and—along with all of the food, including a dozen baguettes, oyster knives, crab crackers, and crab forks—headed across the back country roads to our friends' house, where Christmas lights beckoned from the dark driveway and the smell of a wood fire wafted on the cold night air.

Inside, long tables were decorated with sprigs of red toyon berries and pine branches collected from the nearby canyons, candles glowed from all the nooks and crannies, and a yule log burned brightly in the fireplace, above which the stockings were hung, of course.

Ethel and our French host, Yves, both adept at wielding oyster knives, shucked the bivalves while we drank Champagne and cooked the crabs. It was a memorable evening and a fine introduction for Ethel's new family, who thoroughly enjoyed themselves in spite of the impromptu change of venue.

I love to serve oysters for the holidays, but unlike Ethel, I'm not an adept shucker, so unless she is available with an accomplice to help, I'll serve something else as an appetizer instead, like beef carpaccio, then continue with the crab, a salad, and, if I have the time, a homemade *bûche de noël*. If I'm short on time, I'll purchase one.

Decorating tips: Christmas is one of the easiest occasions for which to decorate. My preference is for red berries, especially those of our local toyon shrub. I mass cedar and pine boughs wherever I can fit them in the dining room, along with pots of blooming amaryllis. I like to use plenty of candles for a soft, cozy feeling and on the table, a pretty table runner scattered with glittery stars.

Cooking tips: Most pastry shops offer special desserts around the holidays, and you could purchase the dessert if you are short on time. If you have a vegetarian guest or two coming to dinner, you can combine this menu with the Holiday Feast of Fruits and Vegetables (page 194): top some of the Belgian endive leaves with shaved Parmesan cheese curls and capers instead of the carpaccio; make a smaller quantity of the Saffron–Root Vegetable Ragout (page 197) to serve in individual serving bowls; add another of the salads; and make or buy a second dessert. Keep the appetizers simple, purchasing items like olives, nuts, smoked salmon, cured meats, or artisan cheeses, and offer them with toasts or crackers.

beef carpaccio curls

Thinly sliced raw beef, simply dressed, is a deliciously indulgent appetizer that suits the holiday season. The watercress adds just enough bite and color, and drizzling it with your best extra-virgin olive oil and a sprinkle of coarse sea salt is all that's needed. Serving the carpaccio on spears of Belgian endive instead of bread or crackers keeps the beef in the foreground, as it should be.

With the tip of a paring knife, remove the core of each Belgian endive by cutting out a cone at the base. Separate the leaves. Each head will yield about 8 large "petals." Reserve the small leaves for another use.

Chill the beef tenderloin in the freezer for at least 1 hour before slicing, or ask your butcher to slice it for you. It should be cut paper-thin, and freezing it slightly beforehand makes the slicing easier.

Arrange the endive petals on a platter, and place a leaf or two or small sprig of watercress on top of each petal. Place a lightly crumpled slice of beef atop the watercress. Repeat with the remaining beef and endive petals. At this point, the appetizers can be covered and refrigerated for up to 8 hours. Just before serving, sprinkle with sea salt and drizzle with a little olive oil.

MAKES ABOUT 40 APPETIZERS, ENOUGH FOR 8 TO 10 SERVINGS

5 heads Belgian endive
1- to 1¼-pound piece beef
  tenderloin
2 bunches watercress, leaves and
  small sprigs only
Coarse sea salt or kosher salt
Extra-virgin olive oil

cracked dungeness crab with
spicy dipping sauce

cracked dungeness crab with spicy dipping sauce

November through May is Dungeness crab season in the San Francisco Bay area, and we feast on them often, buying the crabs live to ensure the best, freshest flavor, and then cooking and cracking them ourselves. However, many people prefer to buy them already cooked and have the fishmonger crack them. Either way, they are an important and delectable part of wintertime menus in our part of the world.

Combine the mayonnaise, ketchup, Worcestershire sauce, onion, pickles, lemon juice, salt, cayenne, and 2 tablespoons of the pickle juice and mix well. Taste and add more pickle juice if necessary. The flavor should be balanced between tangy and spicy, with a hint of sweetness.

Arrange the cracked crab on a platter garnished with the lemons and seaweed, and serve with the spicy dipping sauce.

MAKES ABOUT 3½ CUPS SAUCE, ENOUGH FOR 8 SERVINGS

3 cups mayonnaise

½ cup ketchup

2 tablespoons Worcestershire sauce

2 tablespoons minced onion or shallot

½ cup minced sweet pickles

1 tablespoon freshly squeezed lemon juice, Meyer lemon if possible

¼ teaspoon coarse sea salt or kosher salt

½ teaspoon cayenne

2 to 4 tablespoons sweet pickle juice

3 Dungeness crabs, each about 2½ pounds, cooked and cracked

4 or 5 lemons, cut in quarters lengthwise

Fresh seaweed for garnish, if possible

salad of bitter greens with apple cider balsamic vinaigrette

In August I plant my winter garden, sowing a dozen or more different varieties of escarole, frisée, and radicchio. From November to March, they supply my kitchen with exquisite salads, rewarding me for pulling out the zucchini and eggplants in the summer heat to make room for them.

Rich, dark, sweet apple cider balsamic vinegar, which you can find in specialty stores and at some farmers markets, is, to me, the perfect pairing with the bitter greens, along with olio nuevo, the freshly pressed new olive oil that I buy directly from a mill in November, when the oil is first crushed. It, like the greens, is bitter, but also unctuous, and the balsamic vinegar rounds out the oil's earthy flavor of olive leaves. Of course, you can substitute your usual balsamic vinegar and any good extra-virgin olive oil.

In a salad bowl, mix together the olive oil, balsamic vinegar, red wine vinegar, salt, and pepper with a fork. Taste and adjust with salt and balsamic as necessary. The dressing should be strong and flavorful. Add the radicchio, frisée, escarole, and arugula, and, when ready to serve, toss well.

MAKES 8 SERVINGS

4 tablespoons *olio nuevo* or other extra-virgin olive oil
1½ tablespoons apple cider balsamic vinegar or other balsamic vinegar
½ teaspoon red wine vinegar
½ teaspoon coarse sea salt or kosher salt
¼ teaspoon freshly ground black pepper
1½ cups torn radicchio leaves
2 cups torn frisée leaves
2 cups torn escarole leaves
½ cup baby arugula

hazelnut bûche de noël

My version of the classic French Christmas dessert is very simple—a chocolate sponge cake spread with a chocolate cream filling, rolled up, covered with more of the chocolate cream, and garnished with toasted nuts. For this menu I've chosen hazelnuts, which have a wonderful affinity for chocolate—also they are a nod to Oregon, where many of our hazelnuts are grown, and where my son, Oliver, and his young family live—but frequently I make this cake with local walnuts or almonds. The bûche, *or yule log, should be made no later than Christmas Eve morning, to allow it to chill in the refrigerator. I usually decorate the log with sprigs of toyon berries, pine, or holly, forgoing the traditional meringue mushrooms you'll find if you purchase a* bûche *from a patisserie.*

TO PREPARE THE CAKE

Put the egg yolks in a large bowl and slowly whisk or beat in the sugar until the eggs become thick and pale yellow. Whisk or beat in the cocoa and the vanilla.

In a small bowl, whisk together the flour, baking powder, and salt, and, little by little, whisk or beat this mixture into the egg mixture to form a smooth batter.

In a clean bowl and using a clean, dry whisk or electric mixer, whisk or beat the egg whites until they hold soft peaks.

Preheat the oven to 375°F.

Using a spatula, gently fold the egg whites into the egg yolk mixture.

Line a 10½- by 15½- by 1-inch jelly roll pan with a sheet of kitchen parchment, making sure it rises about ½ to 1 inch above the edges. This will make it easy to remove the roll and peel away the parchment later. Grease the parchment with the butter, being sure to grease the corners well.

CAKE

4 eggs, separated
¾ cup sugar
3 tablespoons good-quality unsweetened cocoa powder
1 teaspoon pure vanilla extract
¾ cup all-purpose flour
½ teaspoon baking powder
¼ teaspoon fine sea salt
½ teaspoon unsalted butter
¼ cup confectioners' sugar

CHOCOLATE CREAM

3 cups heavy cream, chilled
3 tablespoons sugar
6 tablespoons cocoa
¾ cup hazelnuts, toasted, skinned, and finely chopped, plus 6 to 8 whole ones for garnish

With a spatula, spread the batter evenly in the pan. Bake until the cake is puffed and springy when touched, 12 to 13 minutes.

Lay a clean, lint-free cotton or linen kitchen towel on a work surface. Put the confectioners' sugar in a sieve and sprinkle it all over the cloth.

Supporting the cake with one hand, carefully invert the pan onto the towel and release the hot cake onto it. Gently peel away the parchment paper. If any bits of cake come loose, simply stick them back into the cake.

Starting from the long end, roll up the cake in the towel. Once rolled, transfer it to a rack to cool.

TO PREPARE THE CHOCOLATE CREAM

Whip the cream with an electric mixer until soft peaks form. Slowly sprinkle in the sugar and cocoa and continue to whip until the peaks are stiff, 4 to 5 minutes in all.

When the cake is cool, gently unroll it. Spread it with about 1 cup of the filling, going all the way to the edges. Sprinkle with about ¼ cup of the hazelnuts.

Gently roll up the cake again, and place it on the serving platter. Cover the *bûche* completely with the remaining whipped cream, using rough strokes to simulate bark. Sprinkle the cake with the remaining hazelnuts and place the whole nuts along the top. Make a tent of aluminum foil so as not to damage the frosting, and refrigerate the *bûche* for at least 6 hours but no longer than 18 hours until you are ready to serve.

MAKES ONE 15½-CAKE, ENOUGH FOR 8 TO 10 SERVINGS

a holiday feast of fruits and vegetables

CHILLED CRANBERRY SOUP

SAFFRON–ROOT VEGETABLE RAGOUT WITH CRÈME FRAÎCHE AND GREEN HERBS

SALAD OF WATERCRESS AND PARSLEY WITH CHAMPAGNE VINAIGRETTE

QUINCE TARTE TATIN

the party

There are so many delicious fruits and vegetables available in winter that it is easy to make a holiday feast with nary a smidge of meat or fish, and no one will notice it's missing, be they vegetarian or omnivore. Although this is an uncomplicated menu, the presentation can be quite elegant. I like the notion of having a simple starter soup of traditional cranberries, followed by a hearty stew full of roots and Mediterranean flavors. Their essential difference, and this can be emphasized by how they are presented. Part of the fun of entertaining, no matter how small or large the scale, is setting the table and the scene. Delicate French turn-of-the-last-century demitasse cups patterned in crimson that Ethel gave me provide perfect vessels for the soup; I serve the stew in wide-rimmed, contemporary white soup bowls.

Decorating tips: When appropriate, I like to decorate with the fruits and vegetables that reflect the season and the meal. My quinces, which are used to prepare the dessert, also make a beautiful centerpiece, captured under a glass dome and surrounded by holly berries and leaves. Lots of candles—and bits of glass and silver to reflect the warmth of their glow—add to the festive feeling of the meal.

Cooking tips: Offer your guests a glass of Champagne, perhaps with just a drop or two of pear or almond liqueur added to it, when they arrive. I like to always have a bowl of olives and seasoned nuts available to nibble on before dinner. Although your tart can be assembled earlier in the day, bake it after your guests have arrived to ensure that it is served warm and at its best.

chilled cranberry soup

This makes an unusual and colorful beginning to the meal, whetting the appetite for the courses to come. It can be served as an appetizer in a small glass, along with a spoon, or more traditionally, at the table in bowls as a first course.

Combine the cranberries, water, and sugar in a saucepan and bring to a boil. Reduce the heat to medium and cook, stirring, until the berries pop, 10 to 15 minutes. With an immersion blender, purée the mixture.

Transfer the cranberry mixture to a bowl and add half the orange juice and half the orange zest. Let it cool to room temperature, then refrigerate for at least 8 hours, and up to 18 hours, before serving.

Just before serving, stir in the remaining orange juice. Ladle the soup into bowls and garnish with a dollop of mascarpone and a sprinkle of orange zest. Serve immediately.

MAKES 8 SERVINGS

1 pound fresh cranberries, picked over, rinsed, and drained
2 cups water
½ cup sugar
2 cups (about 6 oranges) freshly squeezed orange juice, divided
3 tablespoons (about 1 orange) freshly grated orange zest, divided
½ cup mascarpone

saffron–root vegetable ragout with crème fraîche and green herbs

I am a big fan of root vegetables, with or without meat, and I even wrote a whole book about them. I confess to having loved every minute of my research, and this ragout is a variation on a recipe I developed for that book, Down to Earth. *Root vegetables are quite versatile and adapt well to any flavor profiles. Here, I've used Mediterranean flavors of saffron, garlic, and cumin, and then finished the dish with crème fraîche. Since the olives are salty, taste for seasoning at the end of cooking, adding salt as needed. Serve the ragout with lots of crusty bread.*

Put the saffron threads in the hot water and let stand for 10 to 15 minutes.

Heat the olive oil in a Dutch oven or other deep, heavy-bottomed casserole or pot over medium-high heat. When it is hot, add the onions and sauté until translucent, 2 to 3 minutes. Add the garlic and sauté another minute. Sprinkle in the cumin and black pepper and stir for 1 minute.

Add a little of the broth, stirring to loosen any bits clinging to the pan, then add the remaining broth and the saffron water, and bring the mixture to a boil. Reduce the heat to low and simmer, uncovered, for 30 minutes, allowing the flavors to develop. Add the rutabagas, carrots, parsnips, potatoes, tomatoes with their juices, olives, and salt. Cover and simmer until the vegetables are nearly tender, offering just a little resistance when pierced with a fork, 20 to 30 minutes.

1½ teaspoons saffron threads

1 cup hot water

2 tablespoons extra-virgin olive oil

2 medium-size yellow onions, coarsely chopped

4 cloves garlic, minced

3 teaspoons ground cumin

1 teaspoon freshly ground black pepper

8 cups vegetable broth

½ pound rutabagas, peeled and cut into 1-inch pieces

1 pound carrots, peeled and cut into ½-inch slices

1 pound parsnips, peeled and cut into 1-inch pieces

1 pound potatoes, peeled and cut into 1-inch pieces

1 cup chopped, canned plum tomatoes, with their juices

12 kalamata olives, pitted

½ teaspoon coarse sea salt or kosher salt

2 tablespoons minced mild dried red chile pepper, such as Colorado

(CONTINUED)

Add the chile pepper, kale, oregano, and thyme and simmer until the kale has wilted and is tender, about another 5 minutes. Taste for salt, adding as desired. To serve, ladle the ragout into a soup tureen or serving bowl, swirl with the crème fraîche, and serve hot.

MAKES 8 SERVINGS

2 cups chopped kale
2 tablespoons minced fresh
  oregano leaves
2 tablespoons minced fresh
  thyme leaves
4 tablespoons crème fraîche

salad of watercress and parsley with champagne vinaigrette

The sharp, peppery bite of the watercress makes a good counterbalance to the rich Root Vegetable Ragout. If it seems too intense, replace half the watercress with baby lettuces. For such a special occasion, I would accompany or directly follow the salad with a cheese platter, perhaps including a wedge of Stilton, a Spanish Manchego, and a mild cheese such as Brie or Camembert. The cheese platter could be garnished with dried fruits and nuts, or even a small bowl of honey, which is amazingly good with cheese.

In a salad bowl, combine the olive oil, vinegar, salt, and pepper and mix well with a fork. Place the watercress and parsley on top. This can be done up to 30 minutes in advance. When you are ready to serve, toss the greens well with the dressing.

MAKES 8 SERVINGS

3 tablespoons extra-virgin olive oil

2 tablespoons Champagne vinegar

½ teaspoon coarse sea salt or kosher salt

¼ teaspoon freshly ground black pepper

3 bunches watercress, leaves and small sprigs only, to make about 3 cups

1 cup small whole flat-leaf parsley leaves

quince tarte tatin

This is a recipe from my now out-of-print cookbook, Potager. *It is a wonderful recipe and deserves to have a second life in this book. I now have—I didn't when I wrote* Potager*—a hedge of quince bordering my garden, and each year the bushes bear more and more of the beautiful, fragrant golden fruit.*

I feel so rich to have such an abundance of these old-fashioned fruits, which, while increasingly hard to find here, remain popular in France and Spain, where they are used in both sweet and savory ways. Their season is from late October until December. The quinces are very astringent and essentially inedible when raw, and while they are not very flavorful themselves, they imbibe the flavors of whatever they are cooked with. Here, they are marinated in sugary wine syrup before being baked in the tart.

TO PREPARE THE QUINCE FILLING

Peel and core the quinces and cut them into slices about ⅜ inch thick. In a large bowl, combine the wine, sugar, and vanilla bean. Add the quinces and raisins. Cover and let the quinces marinate overnight at room temperature, turning them several times to ensure an even color.

TO PREPARE THE PASTRY

Combine the flour and salt in a food processor and pulse once or twice. Add the butter and pulse only until pea-sized bits form, about 45 seconds. Add the water 1 tablespoon at a time, pulsing just until a ball of dough forms, about 1 minute. Gather the ball, wrap it in plastic wrap, and chill in the refrigerator for 15 to 30 minutes.

TO ASSEMBLE THE TART

Preheat the oven to 375°F.

Using 1 tablespoon of the butter, heavily butter a baking dish 9 or 10 inches in diameter and 2 to 2½ inches deep. Sprinkle the bottom with ¼ cup of the sugar.

QUINCE FILLING

6 to 8 large, ripe quinces
2 cups merlot, syrah, or a Rhône-style blend
½ cup sugar
One 2-inch piece vanilla bean, slit
1 cup sultana raisins

PASTRY

2 cups all-purpose flour
1 teaspoon sea salt or kosher salt
1 stick plus 3 tablespoons (11 tablespoons total) unsalted butter, chilled and cut into chunks
6 tablespoons ice water

FINISHING THE TART

2 tablespoons unsalted butter, divided
½ cup sugar, divided

With a slotted spoon, remove the quince slices and raisins from the wine marinade. Arrange the quince slices very snugly, making concentric circles in a single layer around the bottom of the dish. Sprinkle a third of the raisins and a third of the remaining sugar over the quince slices. Repeat this entire process twice, but since the second and third layers of quince won't be visible once the tart is inverted, they do not have to be arranged quite as carefully. Cut the remaining butter into small pieces and dot the top of the quince.

On a lightly floured board, roll out the pastry dough ⅛ inch thick and just a little bit larger than the diameter of the baking dish. Drape the pastry over the rolling pin and transfer it to the baking dish. Unfold it and gently place it over the quince, allowing it to droop inside rather than outside the dish. Press the edge of the crust gently against sides of the dish. Lightly prick the pastry all over with a fork. Bake the tart until the crust is golden, and a thick, garnet-colored syrup has formed in the bottom of the baking dish.

When the tart is done, remove it from the oven and let it stand just a few minutes. Run a sharp knife between the pastry crust and the edge of the baking dish to ensure that nothing is sticking. Invert a serving platter on top of the baking dish, and, using a hot pad, hold the platter and the dish firmly together and flip them over, reversing them. The tart will unmold itself onto the platter. Should any slices of quince stick to the bottom of the baking dish, simply replace them on the tart. Serve warm.

MAKES 8 SERVINGS

chinese new year

BITE-SIZE WONTONS FILLED WITH CHOPPED PORK AND WATER CHESTNUTS

GREEN ONION AND GREEN GARLIC PANCAKES

STEAMED BLACK COD WITH HAWAIIAN GINGER

CANDIED KUMQUATS IN SYRUP OVER ALMOND POUND CAKE

table decoration for chinese new year

the party

Living near San Francisco, which has a large and active Chinese American population, I am always aware of the importance of Chinese New Year and its celebrations. One year I had the great pleasure of attending a New Year's banquet where at least fourteen courses were served, each more splendid than the last. That is too much for me to attempt, but it is fun to give a festive dinner to honor the event.

Decorating tips: Since I have a kumquat tree, and kumquats are considered to be lucky for the New Year, I make kumquats a theme of the party, buying dwarf citrus trees for decoration and making a kumquat dessert.

I have a collection of chopsticks that I set out in addition to knives and forks, along with some pretty porcelain Chinese spoons I bought in San Francisco's Chinatown.

Cooking tips: The wontons can be made in the morning, then tightly wrapped in plastic wrap and refrigerated until you are ready to cook them. Do serve the main dish with a big bowl of steamed white rice. To take a shortcut, purchase plain pound cake.

bite-size wontons filled with
chopped pork and water chestnuts

bite-size wontons filled with chopped pork and water chestnuts

These are surprisingly quite quick and easy to make. You can use shrimp instead of the pork, or in combination with it. The problem will be making enough to satisfy the demand for them, once the guests get a taste. Serve these accompanied by small dishes of Chinese chili sauce (available at Asian markets and well-stocked grocery stores), rice wine vinegar, and soy sauce; you can set out individual small bowls for guests to prepare their own dipping sauce from the condiments. The wontons can be served as an hors d'oeuvre or as a first course.

½ pound lean ground pork
8 fresh or canned water chestnuts, peeled and minced if using fresh, drained and minced if canned
2 teaspoons minced garlic
½ teaspoon crushed red pepper flakes
1 tablespoon minced shallots or green onions
1 egg white
½ teaspoon cornstarch
2 teaspoons soy sauce, divided
Dash of sherry
36 round 3-inch wonton wrappers
2 cups chicken broth
4 cups water

Mix together the pork, water chestnuts, garlic, red pepper flakes, shallots, egg white, cornstarch, 1 teaspoon of the soy sauce, and the sherry to make a sticky filling.

Place 1 or 2 teaspoons of filling in the center of each wonton wrapper, and brush a ring of water around the outer perimeter. Gather the wrapper edge upward and inward, and pinch it closed. Set the wonton aside and repeat with the others until all are done.

Put the chicken broth, water, and the remaining soy sauce into a large pot set over medium-high heat and bring it to a boil. Gently slip the wontons into the boiling mixture a few at a time, so they won't be overcrowded. Cook until the wrappers are soft and the mixture inside is opaque, 2 to 3 minutes. Remove the wontons with a slotted spoon and place them on a warm serving platter. Continue cooking them in batches until all are cooked. Serve the wontons hot or warm with toothpicks and preferred dipping sauces.

MAKES 36 APPETIZERS, ENOUGH FOR 8 SERVINGS

green onion and green garlic pancakes

When we think of Chinese food, bread doesn't usually come to mind, but these little fried pancakes make a wonderful bread-based appetizer to serve with the wontons. The pancakes are fun to make because of all the twisting and turning and rolling, which creates the many layers that produce both texture and flavor. By this time of year, my garlic growing in the garden is in its green stage. The garlic bulbs resemble green onions, with beautiful pink-tinged stems, and have a delicate, fresh garlic flavor. They can be found at some farmers markets or in Asian grocery stores. If you can't find them, simply use additional green onions. Serve these accompanied by Chinese chili sauce (available at Asian markets and well-stocked grocery stores), rice wine vinegar, and soy sauce.

4 green garlic bulbs with shoots, if available

4 cups all-purpose flour

½ teaspoon coarse sea salt or kosher salt

2 cups water

10 green onions (14 if you have no green garlic), both white and green parts, minced

3 tablespoons unsalted butter, cut into small pieces

¼ cup peanut oil or canola oil

Trim the tough outer layers of the green garlic bulbs and discard them. Trim back or remove and discard any wilted green tops. Mince the bulb and half of the green tops.

In a large bowl, combine the flour, salt, and water and mix with a wooden spoon or an electric mixer. Turn the dough out onto a lightly floured board and knead by hand for 5 minutes, then let the dough rest for 15 minutes.

Divide the dough into 6 even portions, and, using a rolling pin, roll each into a round about ¼ inch thick. Spread each dough round with about 2 tablespoons of the green onions, a sprinkle of the green garlic, and about a sixth of the butter pieces.

Roll the dough round up snugly and pinch the ends closed. Twist the roll in a corkscrew motion, then stand it on end and flatten it with your hand. The action helps evenly distribute the butter and the filling. Repeat this process with the 5 other rounds of dough, then roll them out again to a thickness of ¼ inch.

Pour enough peanut oil to film the bottom of a medium-size skillet, and heat the oil over medium-high heat. When the oil is hot, place a pancake in the oil and fry until golden brown, about 3 minutes. Turn and cook the other side until golden brown, about 2 minutes, lowering the heat a little bit. Remove the pancake to a paper towel to drain, then put it on a plate or platter in a preheated oven. Repeat with the other pancakes, adding a little more oil if needed as you go. When ready to serve, stack the pancakes on top of each other, and using a sharp knife, cut them into 6 wedges. Serve hot with preferred sauces.

MAKES 6 PANCAKES, ENOUGH FOR 6 TO 8 SERVINGS

steamed black cod with hawaiian ginger

I often grow a selection of Asian greens, such as bok choy, napa cabbage, and mizuna, in my fall and winter garden. I use them in stir-fries and, as in this recipe, for braising. Here the greens are cooked, then the fish steams atop the greens, making for a very delicate yet sophisticated flavor. Serve the fish and greens along with plenty of fresh steamed white rice and extra soy sauce.

Fresh Hawaiian gingerroot (also known as young stem ginger), which is especially tender and fragrant, is used to finish the dish. The gingerroot has very thin pink skin and is available at most Asian groceries and in specialty produce markets.

¼ cup soy sauce

¼ cup dry white wine, such as sauvignon blanc

1 clove garlic, minced

2-inch piece Hawaiian or other fresh gingerroot, peeled and minced, divided

2 heads bok choy, about 2½ pounds

8 black cod fillets, ½ to ¾ inch thick (about 2 pounds total)

In a small bowl, mix together the soy sauce, wine, garlic, and half the ginger.

Coarsely chop the bok choy and rinse in a colander. Lift the greens, still dripping, and put them in a large sauté pan or wok. Place the pan over medium-high heat, add about ½ cup water, and bring to a boil. Cover the pan and reduce the heat to low. Cook the greens until tender, 4 to 5 minutes.

Pour off the liquid from the pan, and stir the soy sauce mixture into the greens. Return the pan to the heat, place the cod fillets on top of the greens, cover the pan, and cook over medium heat until the fish is just opaque, 4 to 5 minutes. Remove the fish to a serving platter and sprinkle with the remaining ginger. Serve immediately.

MAKES 8 SERVINGS

candied kumquats in syrup over almond pound cake

If I don't eat all the tart-sweet fruit right off my kumquat tree, I like to cook some in sugar syrup to use as a dessert sauce. The kumquats are so small that they don't take long to cook, but it does take a bit of time and patience to remove the seeds. You can find fresh kumquats at some produce markets and farmers markets in the winter months. A homemade or purchased almond pound cake is the perfect accompaniment for this treat.

2 cups water
1 cup sugar
¾ pound fresh kumquats, cut into slices, seeds removed
Almond Pound Cake (recipe follows)

In a saucepan over medium-high heat, bring the water and sugar to a boil. Continue to boil, stirring, until a light syrup forms, about 5 minutes. Reduce the heat to medium and add all but 2 tablespoons of the kumquats. Simmer until the skins are translucent, about 5 more minutes.

Let the fruit cool in the syrup. Cover and refrigerate until ready to use, then bring it back to room temperature before serving.

To serve, cut the warm cake into slices ½ inch thick, and place a slice on each of 8 dessert plates. Spoon about ¼ cup of the kumquats in syrup over the cake slices and serve. Garnish with the reserved kumquats.

MAKES 8 SERVINGS

almond pound cake

Almonds are a frequent component in Chinese cooking, and I like pairing their flavor here with the kumquats.

Preheat the oven to 350°F.

Grease a 9- by 5-inch loaf pan with the 1½ teaspoons of butter; set aside.

In a large mixing bowl, beat the remaining butter with an electric mixer until fluffy. Beat in the sugar until well blended, about 1 minute. Add the eggs, one at a time, and beat thoroughly after each one to make a thick, creamy batter. Beat in the almond extract.

In a small bowl, whisk together the flour, baking powder, and salt. Add about one third of the flour mixture to the butter mixture and beat until incorporated. Add a little milk and beat again. Repeat until all of the flour mixture and milk have been added.

Pour the batter into the prepared pan, tapping the pan to settle the batter. Smooth the top of the batter with a spatula.

Bake for 45 to 50 minutes, until the cake has risen and a toothpick inserted into the center comes out clean. Remove the pan to a wire rack and let cool for at least 30 minutes. To remove the cake from the pan, loosen the edges by running a knife along the inside of the pan. Gently turn the cake out into one hand and slip onto a cake plate. Alternatively, slices can be cut directly from the cake pan.

MAKES ONE 9- BY 5-INCH CAKE, ENOUGH FOR 8 SERVINGS

1 cup (2 sticks) plus 1½ teaspoons
   unsalted butter, at
    room temperature
1 cup sugar
4 eggs
1 teaspoon pure almond extract
1½ cups all-purpose flour
1 teaspoon baking powder
½ teaspoon salt
½ cup whole milk

index

Photographs are indicated by italics.

about the author

photograph by Mark Bennington

Georgeanne Brennan is an award-winning cookbook author, with many titles to her credit, including the food memoir *A Pig in Provence*. She divides her time between her home in Provence and her small farm in Northern California, where she gives seasonal cooking classes. Visit her Web site at www.georgeannebrennan.com.